How Can I Find God?

When you search for me, you will find me; if you seek me with all your heart, I will let you find me, says the LORD....

The Book of Jeremiah (29:12–14)

Ask, and it will be given you; search, and you will find; knock, and the door will be opened for you.

The Gospel of Matthew (7:7)

And if [my servant] draws nearer to Me by a handsbreadth, I draw nearer to him by an armslength; and if he draws nearer to Me by an armslength, I draw nearer to him by a fathom; and if he comes to Me walking, I come to him running.

A *hadith qudsi*, a Divine Saying revealed by God through the Prophet Muhammad

This true surpassing single way is
Like a swan's unwavering flight onto a lake,
The Buddha realized in equipoise
And explained repeatedly to groups.
The One who knows the end of birth and death,
The Helper, out of love, teaches
This single path by which all the waters
Were and will be and are being crossed.

From The Tibetan *Dhammapada*, Sayings of the Buddha

Mitakuye Oyasin

Lakota saying used to express one's connection to all creation, both physical and spiritual. Literally: "All of my relatives."

How Can I Find God?

THE FAMOUS AND THE NOT-SO-FAMOUS CONSIDER THE QUINTESSENTIAL QUESTION

EDITED BY JAMES MARTIN

LIGUORI/TRIUMPH
LIGUORI, MISSOURI

Published by Liguori/Triumph
An Imprint of Liguori Publications
Liguori, Missouri
http://www.liguori.org

Imprimi Potest:
The Very Rev. William A. Barry, S.J.
Provincial, The Society of Jesus
New England Province

Library of Congress Cataloging-in-Publication Data

How can I find God? : the famous and the not-so-famous consider the quintessential question / edited by James Martin. — 1st ed.
p. cm.
ISBN 0-7648-0090-6
1. Spiritual biography. 2. Desire for God. I. Martin, James. 1960– .
BL72.H69 1997
291.4'2—dc21 97-7900

Printed in the United States of America
03 02 01 00 99 7 6 5 4 3

For the family into which I was born
and for the one which is mine by profession

CONTENTS

Introduction

It was a quintessentially modern question that was posed to me by a close friend: "How can I find God?"

The question was asked by a young woman who had lost touch with her church. Like many contemporary Americans, while she viewed herself as "non-religious," she admired friends who lived lives of faith, and desired that faith for herself. Still, she was essentially a skeptical woman—intelligent and well educated—living in a secular culture.

It was a real conundrum for her: If you don't have real faith in God, how can you search for God honestly? On the other hand, doesn't the search itself imply faith? Can you somehow "get" faith? She wanted to know if I had any answers for her.

I did the best I could and then decided to ask other people of faith what they might tell my friend.

This book is a collection of those answers, a few of which originally appeared in an article in *America*, the national Catholic magazine. I have tried to include people from as many faith traditions as possible—Catholic, Protestant, Jewish, Muslim, Native American, and Buddhist—and a few who are still searching for one. I have also included people from a wide variety of backgrounds: famous and not-so-famous, rich and poor, young and old, of various ethnic backgrounds from around the country, with the hope that the different types of responses will speak to different readers. My belief is that God is at work in everyone's life, and therefore the comments of a young mother or corporate lawyer or prison inmate are as meaningful as those of a theologian, minister, sister, priest, or rabbi.

Each of the contributors was asked to respond to the following question: If someone were to ask you, "How can I find God?" what would you say? I asked them to imagine the questioner as a close friend, who had no specific religious affiliation. So while the responses often speak strongly of various religious traditions, they can be read by people who do not consider themselves "religious," or even believers.

The contributors to this collection are all North Americans; all but a few are citizens of the United States. Some have migrated to the U.S. from other countries, like Socorro Durán (from Mexico) and Father John Andrew (from England). One, Howard Esbin, is Canadian. Two live abroad: the American novelist David Plante, in London, and Ambassador Jean Kennedy Smith, in Dublin.

There is, however, one exception to this loose rule: Peter-Hans Kolvenbach. Father Kolvenbach, the general superior of the Jesuit Order, contributed a response for the article that appeared in *America*. Originally, I had decided to omit his response for "geographical" reasons. But subsequent to the completion of this manuscript, a friend related how Father Kolvenbach's brief but moving essay helped to dissuade a struggling friend from committing suicide. So that particular essay—from a Dutch Jesuit living in Italy—remains.

To introduce the contributors I have written some short biographies that precede their essays. The "not-so-famous" are afforded slightly longer introductions, on the assumption that you may already know a little more about Elie Wiesel and Mary Higgins Clark than about Deotha Armstrong and Albert White Hat. Often, their life stories are as interesting as their responses: silent clues as to how these people find God in their own lives.

My hope, of course, is that one or more of these essays will draw you closer to God. It is a long journey, but one that, quite obviously, you've already begun.

How Can I Find God?

SISTER HELEN PREJEAN, C.S.J.,

has worked in prison ministry since 1982 as a spiritual adviser with inmates on death row. Her best-selling book, Dead Man Walking, *which is based on her experiences in this ministry, was made into a movie of the same name in 1996. She is a member of the Sisters of St. Joseph of Medaille and lives in Metairie, Louisiana. Sister Helen decided to answer the question orally, and her spirited response is presented here.*

The most direct road that I have found to God is in the faces of poor and struggling people. For me, it was just the connection with people in the St. Thomas housing projects, then with people on death row and in prison, and then with the murder victims' families.

I was forty years old before I realized the connection between the Jesus who had said, "I was in prison and you came to me, I was hungry and you gave me to eat," between that and the real-life experience of being in situations where I was actually with people who *were* hungry and people who *were* in prison and people who *were* struggling with the racism that permeates this society. And it was like the feeling of coming home. Finding God was like coming home, because you just say, "Where have I *been* all my life?"

I remember being in a homeless shelter—a food kitchen. My job was to serve the red Kool-Aid at the beginning of the line when people came for a meal. It was the first conscious act that I did where I needed to be in touch with poor and struggling people. This young man came up, a beautiful kid; he looked like Mr. Joe College. He was handsome, with blond hair and blue eyes, and his hand was shaking as he handed me the cup. And he whispered, "You have to help me, it's my first time here." The tears welled up in my eyes just from being touched. I was thinking, *My God, what is this young guy* doing *here?* It draws out of you this tremendous energy and gifts that you don't even know you have.

My image of finding God is that our little boats are always on the river. We often are in a stall, and we wait and nothing moves, and everything seems the same in life. But when we get involved in a situation like this—for me it was to be involved with poor people—it's like our boat begins to *move* on this current. The wind starts whistling through our hair, and the energy and life is there. And that brought me straight into the execution chamber. You see, it was very quick from getting involved with poor people in the St. Thomas housing projects to writing to a man on death row, to visiting a man on death row, and then being there for him at the end, because he had no one to be there with him. And that experience of being there with him, it's really life up against it: It's life or death. It's compassion or vengeance. All of life is just distilled to its essence.

In that situation, I experienced a tremendous strength and presence of God, that God was in this man that society wanted to throw away and kill. And the words of Jesus that "the last will be first" came home to me. That's what those words meant: that God dwells in the people in the community that we most want to throw away. It's what builds the human family and human community. Because what makes things like the death penalty possible, what makes things like the racism that continues in our society, the oppression of the poor, is that there's this disconnection with people.

To me, to find God is to find the whole human family. *No one* can be disconnected from us. Which is another way of talking about the Body of Christ. That we are all part of this together.

And I feel that *everybody* needs to be in contact with poor people. That in fact, as Jim Wallis of *Sojourners* magazine has said, we need to accept that one of the spiritual disciplines—just like reading the Scriptures and praying and liturgy—is physical contact with the poor. It's an essential ingredient. If we are never in their presence, if we never eat with them, if we never hear their stories, if we are always separated from them, then I think something really vital is missing.

In fact, I think this is one of the greatest problems in our society today. They say that the most segregated day of the week is Sunday because churches very actively participate in segregation. They have incorporated the same system, and so people go to churches with other people just like them.

The "God part" of us is always the one stepping out over, to walk on the water and to take the risk. To go into places *beyond* the part of us that wants to be safe and secure and with the comfortable and the familiar. Just look at all the spiritual journeys, including the trek through the desert to get to the Promised Land. Jesus saying, "I go before you into Galilee." I think concretely that this journey into God translates into the journey into the housing projects, the poor neighborhoods, the inner city, the places where people have AIDS, death-row inmates, battered women, where the suffering of the human community is going on.

The other thing I would want to add to the whole question of finding God is that the journey, wherever it takes us—to me it has been to the poor and the struggling—must be coupled with a reflection and a centeredness that comes from prayer and meditation. It's very important to assimilate what's happening in our lives. I find that I can't function if I don't have that sense of being at the center of myself and in the soul of my soul, so that I am truly operating from the inside out. And it's important to be very self-directed, because it is so possible to be caught on *other* people's eddies in the river and to get into a stimulus/response type of thing. It's so possible not even to realize that we are really moved by other people's vision of life, other people's insights, other people's agendas and just to be caught on one current to another, that we have no rudder on our own boat.

When you hit something big like this, something you know that's bigger than you—like working for justice in the world, or trying to connect faith with going against powerful and entrenched systems—you have this sense of "Yes, I am doing my part." But then you also need to be able to put it down and let God run the universe, so you can play a clarinet or be with your friends or work in a garden.

To be *whole* is very important. Wholeness, I think, is part of godliness. I don't think it's cleanliness anymore that's next to godliness, I think it's wholeness! To have a well-rounded life. To have a good intellectual life, where you're reading and thinking and discussing. To have a strong emotional life where you can give and receive intimacy with people. To develop friendships like a garden. Because there's just no room for these Lone Rangers who go and try to save the world by themselves!

CHRIS ERICKSON

works on the farm that has been in his family for over one hundred years. His ancestors emigrated from Sweden, settling in Nebraska in 1884. On his farm Chris grows 2,000 acres of corn, 100 of alfalfa, and 50 of wheat. Chris' education, a degree in agricultural economics from the University of Nebraska, and his family's experience have helped him to maintain a profitable livelihood, and one that he enjoys. "As a farmer, you're your own boss and can make your own decisions," he says. "Plus, I love working outside."

Chris, thirty-three, was raised as a Lutheran and continues to attend church on a regular basis in his hometown of Holdrege, Nebraska.

If someone were to ask how to find God, I would smile and tell them that I see God every day. Being a farmer requires one to work with the earth and nature, and I cannot think of one occupation outside the clergy that would expose a person to God and His Creation more than farming. From the planting of the seeds through the harvesting of the grain, I see God's plan at work all the time. The complexity and magnificent aura of nature, as well as the constant order under which it functions, leads me to believe that only a Supreme Being could have come up with the idea for its existence.

I also see God in people: These may be people I work with,

do business with, worship with, or friends who I share spare time with. What better source for finding God than people? For we are created after His likeness. God is evident all around us and is easy to find, but in order to do this, one must first have faith in God. Without faith it can be difficult to find God.

To be a Christian requires an act of faith. My own faith has grown through my life, and God's presence has become much clearer. I see Him in the daily work I do as a farmer.

Farming can be a very labor-intensive occupation. Many long, hard hours are spent planting the seeds, tilling the fields, watering the crops, and harvesting the grain. But I have nothing to do with the seeds sprouting, the plant growing, or the production of grain that occurs within the plant. When God created the Earth, He had a master plan for how nature would work. Humans can't make seeds sprout or plants grow; it is God's plan through nature that does the work. All of this is a continuation of my personal relationship with God. In that relationship, faith is the key factor. When I plant the seeds, I have faith they will sprout. If I irrigate the plants, I have faith they will grow. Being a farmer allows me to experience God's Creation and my relationship with Him on both a physical and spiritual basis.

My assumptions of God's presence in nature are based on the fact that God created the Heavens and the Earth. Though I am no expert on the scientific origins of the Earth, I find it difficult to believe that Creation was just something that "happened." The complexity that occurs in nature leads me to believe that a Higher Being had responsibility. The intricate way in which matter is formed, via numerous bonding processes of atoms and molecules and the complexity of genes and chromosomes in animals and humans, demonstrates to me that only a highly intelligent Being could have been the architect of our universe. There is also an order to Creation. The law of gravity, the sunrise and sunset, and the seasonal changes are just a few examples of the orderly way in which the Earth functions. All of this, combined with the magnificent glory of God's Creation, such as the natural beauty of the land and sky, and the vastness of the oceans, makes me believe that God is our Creator, as is described in Genesis.

How can we find God? He is all around us. The essence of our very existence. When we look at God's Creation, we see the wonderful work of the Almighty Hand. I find God in the soil I till, the crops I grow, and the water I use—all working together to provide food for many around the world and myself with a living. I see God in other people through their acts of kindness and caring. And I believe you can find God in the way our universe functions, in the intricate and magnificent way it operates and the consistent order with which it functions—all of which point to God as its Creator. If you have faith, all you have to do is open your eyes, and God is easy to find.

Ron Hansen,

who lives in Cupertino, California, is author of the novels Mariette in Ecstasy, *about the religious experiences of a young nun, and* Atticus. *His short stories are collected in a volume entitled* Nebraska. *In 1989 he received an Award in Literature from the American Academy and Institute of Arts and Letters for his writing. Mr. Hansen, who has recently married, is the Gerard Manley Hopkins Professor of Creative Writing at Santa Clara University.*

"Unfortunately," he wrote in his letter, "I have no unusual insights, only those suggested by a Catholic education."

The first and foremost way of finding God for me is in the Eucharist and in other sacraments and rites. Meditation on scripture, especially the psalms and the gospel accounts of the public ministry of Jesus, has often afforded me overpowering experiences of God's abiding presence, mercy, and love. Retreats, when I can be alone and silent for a while, have been wonderful occasions for getting rid of the turbulence and chatter that interfere with God's efforts at communication. I have profited from using as intermediaries in prayer holy people who have died—Thérèse of Lisieux, Thomas Merton, or Gerard Manley Hopkins—when I need a human face and life to focus on. I also try to hear and see God in friends and family, and to look for the glorious signs of the Holy Being in nature and the sea. And finally, when I write and I have no idea of the origin of a particular scene or image, I like to presume that the Creator is using me as an instrument; and I am humbled, grateful, and thrilled.

Rabbi Michael Lerner

is the founder and editor of Tikkun *magazine, a bimonthly Jewish critique of culture, politics, and society. He is also the author of* Jewish Renewal *and* The Politics of Meaning. *Rabbi Lerner, who holds doctorates in philosophy and clinical psychology, lives in New York City.*

Find God by becoming a partner with God in healing, repairing and transforming the world. Don't look for God, but become Her ally and She will find you.

Don't expect to encounter God as another thing in the world, or as a being who is going to knock on your door or appear in your dreams. Instead, expect to encounter God's presence as the world grows more open to experiencing Her presence.

The entire world is filled with that presence. Writers of psalms could find God everywhere. God hasn't withdrawn. But we have.

The sound waves from God's revelation are still reverberating through the universe. We need to find ways to open our ears.

But that is not easy to do. There are all kinds of obstacles.

It's difficult to hear God's voice, or encounter God's presence, when one is filled with fear and pain. The more we can heal the pain and reduce the fear, the more we will connect with God's presence.

So let's start with a few key elements. End the violence. Stop the process by which some people, armed with the tools of coercion (be they military, economic, or communication and indoctrination), manage to expropriate for themselves a disproportionate amount of the world's resources and wealth, leaving the rest of the world to fend for themselves with inadequate material supplies. End the rape of the natural environment by corporations seeking to maximize profits or by governmental and private enterprises looking at the world as a "resource" to be used rather than as our life-support system to be protected. End hunger and homelessness. Provide for one another's physical needs.

Treat other human beings as if you believed that they were created in the image of God. Recognize them as precious, unique, and yet wonderful, most of all for what they share in common with one another—their capacities for love, caring, intelligence, freedom, creating beauty, and responding to the glory of the universe. Hurry to promote tenderness and gentleness throughout all human interactions, and speedily find strategies to undermine the tendencies of people to blame themselves and feel unworthy. Suffuse the world with loving energy.

Build an economic and political world that tends to reward loving and caring behavior and that supports human beings to go for their "meaning needs," not just for their economic well-being. Build and support communities of meaning that connect people to a higher ethical and spiritual goal than the "looking out for number one" ethos of the contemporary world. Challenge cynicism and defeatism, and encourage people to use their energies in pursuit of the deepest visions of the world they really want.

Build social movements filled with people who are compassionate toward one another and toward those who have not yet accepted the goals of their movement. And let that compassion spread out in every direction—inward toward one's self and toward one's parents and friends, outward toward those who appear to be "the other."

While doing this, take off every Sabbath and spend that entire day celebrating and standing in awe of the grandeur of the universe. Have nothing to do with any other goals on that day. Don't deal with money, or "power over." Instead, only respond with joy and with amazement. Open yourself to that which is beyond categories and that which cannot be fully expressed in language. Go inward, but also go outward. Expand your consciousness. Make this day a day of communal celebration, but also take many hours totally by yourself for inward meditation or outward joy.

Raise children.

Teach them that there is a Power in the universe that makes for the possibility of healing and transformation, and that that Power is what others mean when they talk about God. Become increasingly aware of the ways in which that Power permeates all being, and is the One that is the unity of all. Whenever you look at any reality, acknowledge the God energy. Always be aware of the ways in which *that which is* is in the process of becoming *that which ought to be*, and make yourself part of that process. Never accept reality as it is, because that is the ultimate idolatry. Instead, always affirm to yourself the way the world should and could be different, and help make that happen.

If you spend your days following this path, you will encounter God and She will encounter you.

"But this path requires so much change in the world," you might say, "and so much cooperation with others. I want to find God on my own, and not as part of some larger community or process." It is a fine objection, and quintessentially the expression of the contemporary individualism and alienation from each other that deforms the contemporary world. Part of finding God is learning how to overcome that consciousness and learning to see oneself as part of a much larger whole, one's own consciousness as partial, and one's own needs as partial. When we become aware of the way that so many partial realities put themselves and their needs forward as though they were the center of the universe, we begin to reconstitute ourselves in ways that make us understand that being part of the totality is not necessarily subordination but fulfillment, not necessarily losing oneself but becoming more fully oneself. We can only hear God's voice to the extent that we become more comfortable *not* being the center of the universe, and *not* imagining that we deserve to be encountered totally on our own and somehow totally independent of the world and the community in which we live. Overcome the distortions of ego and alienation, allow yourself to be part, and God's presence will become more apparent.

Pheme Perkins

is professor of theology at Boston College in Chestnut Hill, Massachusetts. An expert on the Gospel of John, she is the author of a number of books, including Reading the New Testament *and* Gnosticism and the New Testament.

The question "How do I find God?" presumes that "God" is missing somehow. Of course, there are times in the spiritual life when God's presence is missing—a rather normal state of affairs if mystics *et al.* are to be believed. Presuming that one has a reasonable practice of private prayer/meditation, communal liturgical worship, study and service, then dealing with the "missing God" is more or less a matter of "waiting it out"—sort of like a heat wave. God'll be back. Probably with a new challenge… so it's just as likely to be the case that finding God is not the problem…God's more like the nasty black fly behind my ear when jogging. How to get rid of God?

Mimi Kennedy

is an actress, a wife, a mother, and a writer. After graduating from Smith College, she moved to New York, making her Broadway debut in Grease *during its original run in the mid-seventies. Her television career began in 1976 with a leading role in a musical series called* Three Girls Three. *Since then, Ms. Kennedy has appeared on television many times, starred as Ruth Sloan in the television series* Homefront, *and was featured in* Savannah. *She has appeared in a number of made-for-television movies, including* Robert Kennedy and His Times *and the Disney Halloween-perennials* Mr. Boogedy *and* Bride of Boogedy. *Her film roles run the gamut from one line in the opening shot of* Death Becomes Her *to Christian Slater's mother in* Pump Up the Volume.

As a writer, Ms. Kennedy was the story editor during the 1990-1991 season of Knots Landing. *Her autobiography,* Taken to the Stage, *which details not only her professional and family history but also the influence of her religious faith, was published in 1996. Ms. Kennedy and her husband, Larry Dilg, live with their two children in Van Nuys, California.*

You can try calling on Saint Anthony, the patron saint of Lost Things, who serves my family even when its members invoke him as pure voodoo. I don't offer this entirely as a glib Catholic joke. It hints at my real answer: Call God, bravely and insistently, and God will find you.

When my father lay dying, surprised and terrified by a massive stroke, I remembered the words to the Saint Anthony prayer. He'd typed it out long ago, on a small piece of paper for me to carry in my wallet. "Come to our aid in the hour of death" it said, I recalled suddenly, and "in that dreadful moment…let us experience thy powerful help." It was his own father's early death that led, I think, to Daddy's lifelong devotion to Saint Anthony. "I lost my father when I was seven" was his invariable description of that tragedy, and if the phrase haunted his childhood the way it haunted him later on, it's not hard to imagine why the Finder of Lost Things became his special friend. Anthony, the monk with the baby in his arms, would have seemed a powerful protector to the boy grief-stricken—and probably guilty—about having unwittingly lost a parent.

"Call Saint Anthony, Daddy," I urged as he struggled on the hospital gurney. "You said that prayer all your life, and it asked for help at the hour of death: *In that dreadful moment.* Call Saint Anthony, Daddy, you have the right." My father calmed. By the time he died an hour later, I thought it seemed he'd recovered everything, including God.

I was given a map of how to find God in my childhood: *The Baltimore Catechism.* It worked while I was in parochial school. But when my point of departure changed—to secular college, then New York City theater—the *Catechism*'s orthodox road disappeared. By then I didn't care; I disdained the God accessible only by fervent Roman Catholics.

When I was lonely and frightened enough, I would call God in long, tearful prayers: Where are You now? Have I sinned too much to know? Let me find You! God sent answers, which I grabbed and then ran with, hardly bothering with thanks for either inner consolation or the earthly rewards I'd begged. The greatest graces I received—being spared much of the harm that could have befallen me in my heedless days—I barely noticed. What did impress me were dazzling coincidences like the fact that I won the role delivering me to "overnight stardom"—top honors in my world of fabulous illusion—the same day I'd scheduled my first spiritual retreat since high school. I glimpsed God in my relationships with other people, though not always as consolation and joy. Sometimes harsh instruction and bitter disappointment seemed the work of Divine intervention.

Not until marriage was I in the same place—mentally, physically, and emotionally—long enough to be addressed by God profoundly. I was finally regularly accessible, and God showed that the Divine Presence is constant. In co-creating children with God and my husband, I learned that the passionate nurture I lavished on my babies was a reflection of the loving care God had lavished on me all along. I understood why "love one another" was the parting commandment of Jesus, the Person by Whom I've known God the longest: Creation needs passionate human nurture to survive. Failure to nurture is the sin of omission by which humanity causes itself and its Creator the most terrible grief.

I've always found it incredible that Mary Magdalene mistook the risen Jesus for the gardener on Easter morning, and that the disciples on the road to Emmaus thought Him a stranger until He broke bread. Was Jesus playing trickster with his risen Body? Were his followers so besotted with grief, so mystically blind, that their senses lied to them? Whatever the intriguing astral complications, the message is clear: Jesus was suggesting to His followers that, after the Resurrection, He would be found in the presence of ordinary people. "The risen Christ dwells with the living. Why seek ye Him among the dead?"

Obey God's commandments. Feed God's sheep. Call God, and make sure there's at least one place where you can always be reached. Check in for messages. God will find you.

Robert Coles, M.D.,

a noted child psychiatrist, is James Agee Professor of Social Ethics at Harvard University in Cambridge, Massachusetts. Dr. Coles is the author of many books, including the Children in Crisis *series (for which he won a Pulitzer Prize) as well as* The Spiritual Life of Children, The Call of Service *and* Dorothy Day: A Radical Devotion.

We find God, I think, through others—through the love we learn to offer them, through the love we learn to receive from them—no small achievement, and indeed, a lifelong effort. We find God with difficulty—the obstacle of pride is always there, with its various forms of expression: self-preoccupation, self-importance, smugness, arrogance, pretentiousness, in George Eliot's phrase "unreflecting egoism"—all of that hinders, squelches the movement of the mind, heart, and soul outward, toward others, whom we might come to know, trust, love, were we less locked into the prison of the self. God, then, is the great Other, and comes to each of us, lives for each of us, insofar as we can find Him through our daily lives: how they are lived with our fellow human beings.

Clifford Stoll

is an astronomer and bestselling author. Dr. Stoll received his Ph.D. for research in Jupiter's atmosphere, from the University of Arizona, where in 1974 he had hitchhiked, as he says, "with big hopes and little money." He has worked as an astronomer at Kitt Peak Observatory in Tucson, and the Purple Mountain Observatory in China. From 1982 to 1985 he built image processing software for the Space Telescope at Johns Hopkins University in Baltimore. Later, he helped to design the optical system of the Keck Observatory, the world's largest telescope, in Mauna Kea, Hawaii.

From 1986 to 1987 Dr. Stoll tracked a computer hacker through a maze of networks, silently watching him as he broke in to forty military computers. After a yearlong chase, involving an electronic sting operation, he tracked him to Germany. There Dr. Stoll and his colleagues discovered a ring of hackers selling military equipment to the KGB. Perhaps not surprisingly, Dr. Stoll's first book, The Cuckoo's Egg, *was a story about computer espionage. His second,* Silicon Snake Oil, *explored the hyperbole and overselling of the information highway. Today he lives with his family in Oakland, California.*

Hey—I'm an astronomer. I'm paid to look at the heavens. Hardly a license to tell you where to seek God.

Likely, you expect me to describe how God is hidden behind h-bar, the Heisenberg uncertainty constant. Or maybe just beyond our finite yet unbounded universe. Indeed, there's plenty of unknowns within the singularities of black holes.

Or come over to my backyard—with my telescope, we'll explore the rings of Saturn, the craters on the moon, and four moons of Jupiter. Hard to find many more beautiful sights in the heavens. Better yet, just look around our own planet: the only place around where you'll find water simultaneously as a gas, liquid, and solid.

But these places and non-places aren't God…nor do I think they'll bring you to God. Despite my yearning to be closer to the skies, I suspect you're asking the wrong person.

For I find God in both equation and eyepiece. As an astronomer, I watch the heavens, but am no closer to the Creator than a physician is to your soul. All the more reason to find a companion in your search…perhaps someone who views our heavens through a different lens.

And while I know plenty about our physical universe, I'm left with a profound wonder at how much is left to discover. The glow of a sunset gives a joy quite inexplicable by my knowledge of radiative transfer. Holding a newborn against my chest brings a happiness that transcends my understanding of biology.

It makes me wonder about beginnings and endings. Did God tweak the early solar nebula to give Earth just the right composition, temperature, and pressure for people to thrive? Is a Supreme Being watching our struggles and evolution? Might these physical wonders and questions have been created for my enjoyment to explore?

Better that you start your search for God with the wise, not the clever. For information, check into the newspapers, magazines, television, or the Internet. For knowledge, open a text on radiative transfer or an introduction to celestial mechanics. But for wisdom, look to the Talmud, the Bible, the Quran, the Tao Te Ching, the Sama Veda, and the Vinaya Pitaka.

Find a quiet place and read what's happened before and how others grappled with the infinite. Astronomy and science may be an expression of your search, but I suspect the skies alone won't hold the answer.

HON. JEAN KENNEDY SMITH

is the U.S. ambassador to Ireland, appointed to this post by President Bill Clinton in 1993. In 1974 Mrs. Smith founded Very Special Arts, an educational organization affiliated with the John F. Kennedy Center for the Performing Arts, which provides artistic opportunities for individuals with mental and physical disabilities. Very Special Arts has affiliates in all fifty states and in over seventy countries around the world. Ambassador Smith currently lives in Dublin, Ireland.

If someone were to ask me about finding God, I would start my answer by reflecting on the values which were taught to me by my parents. My parents were generous and loving, and their faith helped to shape all of their children as individuals and as a family. In our home, faith and prayer were important values, and, as the years went on, Mother established the tradition of all the family saying the rosary together on special occasions or, sometimes, just sitting on the porch after dinner. Through her example, Mother showed us that prayer was part of our everyday lives—that it was important to attend church on Sunday, but that it was equally important to stop in for a visit when we were shopping in town. In that way, we came to think of religion as a conscious search, rather than an authoritative demand, as something that enriches our life, rather than restricts it.

Over the years, I have become more and more aware of the

many different ways in which one can search for God. There is no single path. In my work with artists, some who have overcome significant physical and mental challenges, I have often been impressed by the way in which they have found grace through their artistic expression. Through the arts, possibly unlike any experience, a person is able to transcend limitations, explore the imagination, and discover the unknown. This process of discovery can awaken for all of us the profound wonders and the deep meaning in our lives.

The knowledge that spirituality reveals itself in many diverse places and forms has made me more aware of the intrinsic value of the different religions throughout our world. In my life, I have been privileged to witness a variety of religious traditions, each with its own richness and beauty, each marked by prayer and fidelity as pathmarks which point toward God.

I think that we all need to realize that God and the search for faith are truly universal, and that there are many ways to express belief and to search for that which lies beyond. Our search for God is, I think, a search for a better humanity, one in which there is love and compassion for all people. It must be rooted in these values and marked by an openness and understanding of the diversity of human expression.

RICHARD J. MOUW, PH.D.,

is president of Fuller Theological Seminary. Based in Pasadena, California, Fuller is the largest interdenominational seminary in the world. Dr. Mouw joined the faculty of Fuller in 1985 as professor of Christian ethics. Prior to this, he served for seventeen years as professor of philosophy at Calvin College in Grand Rapids, Michigan. He is the author of ten books, most recently Consulting the Faithful.

Dr. Mouw and his wife, Phyllis, an art historian, live in La Cañada, California, and are members of the La Cañada Presbyterian Church.

I usually don't expect to get my theological insights from bumper stickers, but a few years ago I saw one with a message that struck me as profound: "You are a child of God. Please call home." That's as good an answer as any I can think of to the "How can I find God" question.

The "home" image expresses a basic motif in the biblical portrayal of our human quest for spiritual fulfillment. To "live in the shelter of the Most High" (Psalm 91:1) is to find our only place of genuine safety and nurture. This is the abiding place where all human restlessness finds its peace.

I am not very pluralistic in my understanding of where we are to find ultimate fulfillment for our spiritual strivings. If we take the biblical story seriously we have to insist that there is really only one true Home, and that the search for God, if it is to be a successful one, must aim in that direction: the embrace of the God who has drawn near to us in Jesus Christ.

My own conviction that the journey to God must eventually pass through the Stations of the Cross grows stronger all the time. But I also find myself regularly humbled by the recognition that finding God is very much a process, a journey with many twists and turns. We have a long way to go before we arrive. "What we will be has not yet been revealed. What we do know is this: when he is revealed, we will be like him, for we will see him as he is." (1 John 3:2)

I am also regularly surprised by the different routes people take in moving toward Home. I had a student a few years ago who came to seminary after a very profound conversion. She had grown up in a very secular environment and in her young adulthood had been attracted to a New Age cult. She joined a commune led by a guru who gave each member the assignment of studying a great religious teacher. She was assigned to Jesus, and began to read the gospels. She was intrigued, but she was also disturbed by what she felt were differences between what the New Testament affirmed and what she was being taught in the commune. Her guru told her not to worry: She must simply embrace all that she was learning from her assigned teacher. One Sunday she attended a church service. She never went back to the commune. Today she is an evangelical pastor.

The religious pluralists are right in one sense: There are indeed many paths to take on the search for God—even though I find it necessary to name the One who alone can guide us to our destination. My own pilgrimage toward finding God is greatly enriched by hearing the stories of other journeys, other paths. Indeed, it is in the sharing of those stories, with all the courageous accounts of "many dangers, toils and snares" that have been encountered along the way, that I experience the profound contours of the *communio sanctorum*: a company of pilgrims who have not yet arrived, but who have been given, by God's grace, powerful intimations of what it will mean to arrive at Home.

KATHLEEN HASER

has been the director of Jesuit Volunteer Corps: East since 1983. The Jesuit Volunteer Corps is an organization that enables recent college graduates to work directly with the poor in inner cities, while integrating their religious faith.

Kate's faith has always been important to her. "I've been going to Mass every day since I was twelve," she explains. "For me, it's just part of life." After graduating from the University of Maryland in 1969 Kate worked in public relations and, for five years, with American Film *magazine at the Kennedy Center in Washington, D.C. Her current job in Philadelphia allows her to combine her religious commitment with a professional career. "I'm able to do an important work of the Church," she says, "and expose college grads to poverty in this country." Recently, Kate spent a sabbatical year at the Weston Jesuit School of Theology in Cambridge, Massachusetts, and participated in a retreat directors' workshop at the Centre for Ignatian Spirituality in Guelph, Ontario.*

How can you find God? In your own life experiences! People of faith live in the belief that God has created them and the world, loves and sustains them, and desires the fullness of life and justice for all. The desire you express is given to you by God, so God has already found you. Take ten minutes at the end of the day and be quiet. Say, "God, help me to know you." Consider your day: when you felt peaceful or most yourself, when your spirit soared or when you were deeply moved by someone's pain. God's there—not as an object to be found, but offering a relationship to enter into. Tell God what you are grateful for. Read through the Psalms until you find one that speaks to you. As you become aware of God's presence in your life, ask your friends who live lives of faith to help you sustain your experience of God.

Chris and Kim Brown

met during their days as undergraduates at Bucknell University in Pennsylvania. They were married a few years later, in 1984. Chris, age thirty-seven, was raised in Princeton, New Jersey, the son of a university professor there. After graduating from Bucknell, Chris accepted a job with General Electric, where he works today. As a portfolio investment manager for GE Investments, Chris makes decisions concerning the types of investments the company's pension plan will make. He loves his work. "It affords me real intellectual stimulation by forcing me to study and learn about a variety of industries, and also appeals to the gambler in me."

Before and for a few years after their marriage, Kim taught at private schools in New Jersey and Connecticut. She is now raising their two young children at their home in Ridgefield, Connecticut. Chris and Kim have recently become very active in the local United Church of Christ church: The First Congregational Church of Ridgefield. Chris serves as head of the board of trustees, and Kim teaches Bible school and works with children in the church community.

CHRIS:

How can I find God? By attending a church. By reading the Bible.

It sounds so simple, but recognize that these are no small tasks. They require an initial, and an ongoing, commitment.

My eleven-year journey to know God began in a beautiful Presbyterian church in central New Jersey. My wife and I were newlyweds, living on Main Street in a small house. I am not really sure why we began attending this particular church. It, too, was on Main Street and the chapel and surrounding grounds dominated the town. I think we were initially drawn more by the architecture than any particular call. But we were immediately taken by the couple who were co-ministers. They each brought a unique style to the pulpit that made us want to attend each subsequent Sunday. They addressed many aspects of everyday life, making their sermons both relevant and practical. They awakened me to a new perspective on life. I could no longer keep the same attitudes and habits that I had prior to beginning my journey.

Early on, one of the ministers introduced me to a daily devotional guide. It was during that time that I began to read a small portion of the Bible each day.

The Bible had always been intimidating to me. A massive text, filled with unpronounceable names and places. I would start at the beginning, read a few chapters from Genesis, but quickly lose interest. But this new approach of reading a selected passage, with an accompanying interpretive text, enabled me to begin to hear the message of Jesus Christ. It was through these nightly readings that my relationship with God became permanent.

It is the Bible that has brought me closer to God, and changed the context in which I lead my life. It is my *Life's Little Instruction Book*. The context for all that I do is now a framework drawn from many different books and passages of the Bible.

Becoming a student of the Bible will force a recognition that there may need to be a lot of change in the way that you do things. Courtesy, compassion, understanding, empathy, sympathy, humility, meekness, love. These are the values that will need to fill your life. Anger must fall away. Covetousness must end. Revenge must be replaced by forgiveness.

But be careful what you wish for. It's not going to be easy. Not too long ago, I sat on a dock bordering one of New Hampshire's lakes with a friend who had recently grown closer to God. She offered, "Isn't it difficult to try to live up to the standards set by the Bible?"

There is no question about it. It is easy to avoid the issues that are raised, to ignore the sin in our lives.

This can all lead to a great disappointment in oneself. Realizing that sin fills our lives is a difficult revelation. There is no little sin: Cheating on an expense account is a sin. Taking a box of paper clips from the office is a sin. But the beauty of finding God is also finding the understanding that we are forgiven for our sins when we profess our faith. And professing our faith will be the first step in moving toward a less sin-filled life.

Having begun to read the Bible, you will soon be able to find God in all that you do. In your home, in your workplace, in your town, in your relationships, you will find the presence of God once you start actively looking for Him. It will change the way you treat other people, the way you approach decision making, the way you handle any situation.

Attending church will then reinforce all that you are reading during the week. Sharing time with fellow believers will be an enriching experience. Hearing the Bible preached from the pulpit will challenge and enlighten you. It will offer a weekly opportunity to recharge your batteries, and fill your spirit with the Word of God. It also provides an opportunity to share your talents toward the betterment of the Church. My own skills are in financial management, and so I have been involved in both stewardship and trustee activities. A particularly challenging stewardship campaign recently taught me much about prayer and myself. We now pray nightly with our children, passing on the lessons that we've learned later in life.

It has been by reading the Bible and attending church that I have found God. Searching for and finding God will bring you a life-altering, everlasting peace. As the Gospel of Matthew says, "Blessed are those who hunger and thirst for righteousness, for they shall be filled" (5:6).

KIM:

Clearly, I recognize that God has different plans for different people. So maybe the easiest way for me to talk about finding God is to tell you how I found God.

Mine is not a story of an overnight transformation. I did not have a blinding conversion like Paul on the road to Damascus. I've always believed in God. It's hard to look around at the beauty of the creation, or into the eyes of my children, and deny that He exists. No, I was always very certain of His existence. But finding the true nature of God and developing a relationship with Him didn't begin until I was in my early thirties.

Like many people, I found Him because I needed Him. I was going through an identity crisis. As far as crises go, this may seem mundane, but this is the way it happened.

I was in my third year of motherhood. All my life I knew I wanted to be an at-home mom. Before having children I had a teaching career that I enjoyed very much. Still, when I became pregnant there was never a question that I would quit my job and stay home to raise my family. When we bought our house, we applied for a mortgage based on my husband's salary alone. Parenthood, and my staying home, was definitely something we planned for. But three years into it, with a three-year-old and a one-year-old, I began to have serious doubts about my decision. I was deep in dirty diapers, ear infections, sleepless nights, and when my daughter came home from nursery school with head lice, it nearly pushed me over the edge. I had totally lost my sense of self, and I was depressed. I didn't like my "job," and although I loved my children, I began to think that this full-time motherhood thing really wasn't for me. For months I moped around, trying to figure out what would make me happy.

Then, all within a few weeks' time, and out of the blue, people from my past started popping up. My best friend from high school called. As we talked about her own struggle with multiple sclerosis and her decision not to risk having children, I felt my perspective on motherhood beginning to change. I was able to have children, and had two beautiful, healthy ones at that.

Then a dear friend from my early teaching days called. She, too, had become a full-time mom, and called to share the joys of motherhood with me. But instead of harping on the negative, which I had become so accustomed to, she talked about the wonders of childhood. How privileged we were to be there for the first step, the first words, each new discovery. My perspective altered a little more.

Next, a college friend and his wife came for lunch one day. They didn't have children, but were hoping to start a family soon. The conversation quickly took my usual negative tack, as I lamented how difficult it was to be at home. The wife was in full agreement with me, and talked about how there was no way that children would make her give up her career. She felt day care or a nanny was definitely the way to go. But hearing her echo my sentiments actually startled me. It made me think, "Wait! Do you really want someone else to raise your children?"

It was the call from my church, though, that was like a blow to the head. This wasn't a call from my past, it was someone from the present who was answering my immediate need. It became clear to me that there was some Divine intervention going on. The women's fellowship called to see if I might be interested in leading a monthly meeting for a small group of moms with young children. Childcare would be arranged during the meetings, and the programming would be my choice. Here was an opportunity to do something to enrich myself. I could feel the creative brain cells starting to rev up; I would have to call upon those "lost" organizational skills, and, most importantly, I would gain support from other women in my position. And it was all within the realm of my at-home mom job. It was perfect. I am an occasional journal writer, and on the day that call came I wrote, "Perhaps this is the answer to my prayers, and I didn't even realize I had been praying." Leave it to God to state the obvious through a call from the church.

That's how it began. Through all those people and finally through a call from the church, I found God. He was there all along, of course. I just finally recognized how ever-present He was and is. I could see Him helping me through my "crisis."

I have a favorite Scripture quote from Revelation 3:20, "Here I am! I stand at the door and knock. If anyone hears my voice and opens the door, I will come in and eat with him, and he with me." It was slow in coming, but I finally heard God's voice, and I let Him in. Now that I have found God, it is easy for me to look back and see how His perfect plan for me has unfolded. I see that He planned for me to be a full-time mom. God put everything in place so I could be just that. And when I struggled, I see how He heard my cries for help, and answered. Each day, if I rely on Him, He helps me find joy in my "job," my children, my life.

Relying on God and trusting Him with everything is, of course, the tricky part. Every day I have to open that door and let Him in, and let Him show me what He has planned. Since I started my walk with the Lord, I have faced many tests of faith and trust, but it would probably take another dozen pages to show you how He has pulled me through each time! Maybe that can be the title of the next book: *How to Trust God.*

God bless all who are looking for Him. He's just on the other side of the door.

PAUL GOULET

discovered a few years ago that he had contracted the HIV virus. As a result, he decided to leave his job with a consulting firm in Boston to work full time as a volunteer in various charitable groups. Previously, Paul had worked for seven years at MIT helping to automate the library of the Sloan School of Management.

Today, Paul spends much of his time educating high school and college students about AIDS, and has won several corporate philanthropic awards in recognition of his work. He volunteers for Victory Programs, an agency that provides alcohol and drug-treatment programs, education and housing for poor people with HIV/AIDS. Paul says his volunteer work has been "a big boost psychologically and spiritually for me." He is also one of the founders of the Last Tuesday Dinner Program in Boston, an organization that serves dinners (on the last Tuesday of each month) to 125 people with AIDS and their families.

Several years ago I was admitted to an emergency room with a diagnosis of a stroke. I had not spent much time in hospitals previous to my HIV diagnosis, so the experience was pretty frightening. If there was ever a time when I was looking for God it was then. Several of my friends were notified that I was in the hospital, including my best friend, Bill. Bill had been diagnosed with AIDS several years before and now his condition had worsened. He had Kaposi's sarcoma, and since most of his K.S. was on his feet and legs, he could hardly walk. The previous night we attended a concert for an AIDS benefit and Bill spent most of the night in tears because of the intense pain he was in.

As I was lying in the emergency room the doctors informed me that they needed to perform a lumbar puncture (spinal tap). In the meantime, my partner Danny called Bill to let him know that I was in the hospital and what the doctors wanted to do. I had heard how painful this procedure is and wasn't very excited about the prospects. Now I really needed God but wasn't sure how I would find him in all of my fear and frustration. About thirty minutes later Bill walked into the emergency room and asked where I was.

He immediately entered the room and held my hand, helping me with my pain. At that moment Bill forgot his own pain and let me know that everything would be OK. I often wonder if I would be able to do the same for someone else. I no longer needed to find God; at that moment God was with us in all our pain and fear. I knew I could find God in the human heart, in the form of the love, compassion, and sacrifice that Bill had shown me so beautifully in the simple gesture of holding my hand.

It is not always easy to find God today, especially with all the world's ills and tragedies. How can we find God in AIDS, in violence, in hunger, in poverty, in sickness or in war? What kind of universe, world, God, or life would deliver blows like these to anyone? On a spiritual level these thoughts leave me empty. Seething with anger and rage, I sometimes say, "You tell me where God is in all of this." These are the senseless, tragic, and cruel events that pull that magic carpet out from under us. It's the magic carpet that we sit on through life that allows us to ride out life's events believing that with all the disappointment and pain life is still worth living—and that soon everything will be OK, and somehow God is with us through it all. I've learned that

God doesn't cause these tragedies, but we find God in the human response to them.

I am always amazed that in this world of technological innovation and sophistication my heart can still break. No amount of technology, no amount of innovation can heal me. And when my heart is broken, I can't hear my heart, I can't hear my God.

To find our God we must shift our focus inward, relying on the communications of our hearts. There, in our hearts—our inner voice—is the seat of wisdom that will lead us to our God.

If we fail to listen we will never hear the advice that God offers to you and me at every moment of our lives. I like a line from the *Gospel of Thomas:* "Recognize what is before your eyes, and what is hidden will be revealed to you." Wherever you want to see the face of God you will see it, and if you don't want to see it, no matter—for it is always there.

Rev. Richard P. McBrien

is the Crowley-O'Brien-Walter professor of theology at the University of Notre Dame. He is the author of the widely used textbook Catholicism *and editor of the* HarperCollins Encyclopedia of Catholicism.

I don't believe it is possible for any ordinary mortal, this side of the Beatific Vision, to "find" God directly. I am convinced that honest, searching mainline believers have more in common with agnostics and even some atheists than they do with religious enthusiasts who are certain not only of having "found" God but of knowing precisely "His" mind and will on a wide spectrum of religious, social, political, and economic questions.

To the extent that any of us "finds" God, it is indirectly, not directly. The theological synonym for "indirectly" is "sacramentally." We come to a knowledge and experience of God through others. The invisible God is made visible through the sign of the neighbor. We know God's love, mercy, justice, compassion, and forgiveness through the love, mercy, justice, compassion, and forgiveness that we receive and share with others. That is why St. John reminds us that "Whoever does not love does not know God, for God is love.... Those who say 'I love God,' and hate their brothers or sisters, are liars; for those who do not love a brother or sister whom they have seen, cannot love God whom they have not seen" (1 Jn 4:8,20). Looking for God? Look across, not up.

Rev. Dr. Clifford A. Jones, Sr.,

is the senior minister of the Friendship Missionary Baptist Church, a congregation located in the inner city of Charlotte, North Carolina. A graduate of University of Maryland-Eastern Shore, Dr. Jones worked for many years as a high-school teacher before entering Southeastern Baptist Theological Seminary in 1969. He enjoys his ministry immensely. "The joy of preaching about the Word increases with every opportunity," he remarks. "And a calmness moves and increases in my life as I grow closer to the Word of God."

At Southeastern Baptist, Dr. Jones received both a master's degree in divinity and a master's in theology. He later received his doctor of divinity at the Boston School of Theology. Noted for his achievements in Who's Who Among Black Americans, *he is president of North Carolina's General State Baptist Convention, representing 450,000 Baptists, the majority of whom are African-Americans. He is also president of the Lott Carey Baptist Foreign Mission Convention, which represents eighteen states and the District of Columbia. Dr. Jones and his wife, Carolyn Brenda Reynolds, are the parents of two grown children.*

It is through our hollowness that we have the capacity to be filled. The hollowness and filling is not a one-time experience, but a lifelong journey, along which will come opportunities for our experiencing something special, if only for a moment.

How do you coax a cool breeze to locate you on a steamy, humid, muggy July afternoon when there is no air conditioning available? In North Carolina's Moor Country, Luther, Ada Williams, and Doddy Robert lived in a home that was built on a little hill at the top of their gravel driveway. In the yard were two white oak trees that bore the scars of unfavorable winds and aging. Around ten in the morning, we would occupy familiar chairs, shelling peas, snapping bluelake string beans, discussing the Sunday School lesson, and eating creek-cooled watermelon. Periodically, a cool refreshing breeze would come and find us. At best, we put ourselves in an anticipatory circumstance and postured ourselves to be recipients as cool comfort came by and we thirstily sipped from Divine benevolence and said, "Thank you, Laud."

When I was a child, my mother, who was fondly known as Ms. Cora, my sisters, and I worked during the summer—the latter part of June through the third week of August—picking blueberries on farms in South Jersey. Our days were long, starting at sunrise with my father saying as he awoke, "Joshua rose from his western cot." The day moved slowly. By eleven, it was extremely humid and hot, and remained the same until evening. Looking down those long rows of bluebell blueberries and across those twenty-plus acre farms, no shade to be found, you could see waves of heat like a menacing mirage as far as the eye could see. During these times our mother would say, "Lord, have mercy on your children." In a matter of moments or hours later, in this humid hollow of sweltering heat, a cool refreshing breeze would find us, treating our tired tan bodies, smiling upon sweat-stained brow and cooling our being to the marrow of the bone. In this humid hollow as we were trying to make it, God found and smiled upon us with a refreshing breeze.

My mother, Ms. Cora, would stop picking and look in the

face of the breeze with her refreshed tired smile and say, "The good Master is watching over his poor children; thank you, Lord, for the cool breeze." My mother taught us that God knows the circumstances, and it is we who need to call from the deep with honest integrity all the while thanking God for being on the way. Thank you, Laud!

Finding God necessitates a realization of the needs of others and a willingness to improve their circumstances. There was once an unusual man—both aged and young—whose relationship with God bordered on the absurd of unexplainables: a heavenly voice and a dove during his baptismal experience in a muddy river; questions about his formal training and confirmation; questionable comrades and companions; his unusual relationships with women and children; his odd eating and drinking habits. Yet he was extremely secure in the midst of these hollowing experiences. There are retrospective nit-picky scholars who postulate that God affirmed him at birth. Others argue that it occurred on an obscure hill as he communicated law and prophecy. Others believe this relationship was affirmed during a midnight prayer vigil while his three friends slept and his personal potential possibilities became petitional prayer for the higher will to be done. This hollow of verbal and nonverbal submissiveness of will for Will, feeling broken, forsaken, rejected, and misunderstood postured this aged young man to experience God by placing others before himself. Consequently, his Calvary experience, his dying experience, his pain, his rejection was not "self-ward" nor self-centered. His hollow was filled from his compassionate love for others that conquered the void of personal preference. A cause called to something deeper than the temperate temptation and the secure shadows of the self.

He is the essence of Easter, from whom one is never excluded. Open yourself continually and experience sweet fragrance, tenderness in touch, refreshment in humid fields of despair, a cool breeze on a hill. Call from the honest hollow, as absurd or awkward as it may feel; trust your tired troubling circumstances with him. Ms. Cora will tell you that His presence is there—"Thank you, Laud!" Jesus called out to God from a cross during a humid noonday experience and was placed in a hollow, but God found and empowered him in the hollow, and as "Joshua was raised from his western cot," so Jesus was raised as the Christ. God can be experienced through natural phenomena, the personal experiences of others, but ultimately through a relationship with Jesus Christ. Thank you, Laud.

FREDERICA VON STADE

is an internationally acclaimed mezzo-soprano. Ms. von Stade is a recitalist, opera singer, and recording artist in great demand. She has appeared in most major American and European opera houses and has sung with many of the world's finest orchestras. Her albums, which feature everything from Mozart opera to American musical classics to French art song, include My Funny Valentine: Frederica von Stade Sings Rodgers and Hart; Chants d'Auvergne, *with the Royal Philharmonic; and* Simple Gifts, *with the Mormon Tabernacle Choir. Ms. von Stade lives with her husband in Alameda, California.*

Your question brings my mind to a complete halt, which is somewhat disappointing since I have received so much comfort from my faith throughout my life. From earliest childhood, I have had a deep affection for every aspect of my religion—perhaps as much for its great sense of theater as for its content. Mine is a child's religion to this day, and this is perhaps why it is so difficult to answer your question.

Since my attachment was formed at such a young age, I guess my response would be that you could find God in the Convent of the Sacred Heart, in Bethesda, Maryland, in a chapel filled with incense, kneeling next to a beautiful white candle carefully tied with a lovely ribbon, holding a program in front of your eyes with elegant writing describing the First Communion ceremony of yourself and your classmates. God was delivered to my doorstep from my birth by nuns, priests, and my convert grandmother. So faith was easy and has provided me with one of the greatest comforts and joys of my life.

God is most visible in children, and it is as children that it is easiest to find God, if only we adults can remember to describe and present Him and His family in a lovely, comforting, and safe light. I think this is about as close as I can come to answering your question.

When thinking about God I am always reminded of a wonderful saying I once heard: "Do you know how to make God laugh? Tell Him your plans!" I had not experienced the agony of frustration of dealing with life when it was out of my control until much later in my life. Now, with that experience behind me, I feel even more connected to humanity and am intensely grateful for the experience of having been led through it by my faith.

VEN. BARDOR TULKU RIMPOCHE

is a Buddhist lama who lives at Karma Triyana Dharmachakra monastery, a traditional Buddhist monastery situated in the Catskill Mountains in New York. The monastery is part of the Karma Kagyu tradition, one of the four major lineages of Tibetan Buddhism, all of which trace their origins to the Buddha.

Venerable Rimpoche was born in 1950 in Tibet. From an early age he was tutored by a Dharma *(Buddhism) instructor while living with his family, who were nomads constantly on the move with their animal herds. With the Chinese Communist occupation of Tibet, Rimpoche's family fled to India. His family, a group of fifteen, escaped through the Himalayas and finally descended onto the hot plains of Assam, India. It was there that, when Rimpoche was nine, his entire family died one by one, unable to endure the tropical heat. When his father, the very last member of his family, died, Rimpoche and a group of other Tibetans fled to the town of Bomdila, where the borders of Tibet, Bhutan, and India meet. When the town was bombed, Rimpoche and a twelve-year-old friend fled the attack to Darjeeling.*

After his arrival in Darjeeling, His Holiness, the XVIth Gyalwa Karmapa, the head of the Karma Kagyu lineage, who had earlier recognized the young boy as the reincarnation of the previous Bardor Tulku, arranged for him to be tutored in a monastery in Sikkim. There he began his training as a tulku, *a recognized reincarnate lama, for twelve years. In 1978, at the urging of the Gyalwa Karmapa, Rimpoche opened the monastery in the Catskills, to establish a center for the teaching of Tibetan Buddhism in the United States. There, along with the abbot, he guides and teaches other monks and visitors.*

In 1994 Bardor Tulku Rimpoche became an American citizen. He is married to Sonam Chotsu and has three young daughters.

Buddhist cosmology describes gods and god realms in detail, so in one sense this question can be answered quite literally. In another sense, though, this question could be understood as a question about how to awaken ourselves to what is fundamentally meaningful. In other words, finding God can be addressed either from the letter or spirit of the question; and it may be helpful to do both.

Buddhists acknowledge various god realms, each of which is considered to have every bit as much reality as this human realm. By our human standards, these god realms are permeated by unimaginable pleasure and splendor. The life span of gods is measured in thousands and tens of thousands of years. The gods in these realms embody great beauty and extraordinary powers that result from their having cultivated vast merit and positive *karma* (actions) in their past lives. It requires an enormous amount of merit to be reborn in the god realms; and, not surprisingly, the god realms are not overly crowded.

The point is that one could come to experience these god realms or even be born as a god just as others have done, by accumulating a similar wealth of positive actions. Despite how attractive such a rebirth may seem, however, beings in the god realms are still subject to impermanence and change. This is because each is still at least somewhat tainted by emotional obscurations such as pride or jealousy. These conflicting emotions prevent even gods from obtaining the complete liberation and freedom of Buddhahood. It is because of this that Buddhists would more likely interpret the concern for finding God as a figurative expression of the concern for realizing the Ultimate Source of meaning in one's life.

When someone asks fundamental questions about the nature of her or his life, it is a cause for some celebration. It suggests that at least for that moment the person has paused sufficiently from ordinary busyness and mundane preoccupations to reflect on what it means to be alive. So, from this point of view, the question is considered very auspicious.

I would certainly encourage anyone who takes such a reflective stance with regard to his or her life not to lose such an interest, but to deepen it by examining what is most important for his or her own life. I would also suggest that the person broaden his or her understanding by taking note of how other people lead their lives as well. The one thing that will become abundantly clear is that we all want to be happy and to avoid suffering. The fundamental need to find happiness characterizes all sentient beings. We are not talking here about superficial pleasures or temporary distractions; rather, we are talking about the underlying desire for genuine and lasting happiness and abiding protection from suffering. To give an extreme illustration, even a person who contemplates suicide does so because of an overwhelming desire to be free of suffering. It is not just in the extreme examples, though, that we find this underlying motivation.

The desire for happiness permeates our everyday activity, and that is why we are all so busy. We work, study, marry, divorce, make friends, fend off enemies, party, vacation, shop, save, and play. This does not mean that our busyness leads to happiness. On the contrary, it often makes us miserable. It does illustrate, however, that the desire for happiness underlies everything that we do. Not only do we all want happiness and freedom from suffering; we all want it one hundred percent. The search for happiness is never a halfway sort of thing. It is in fact this boundless drive that gives rise to these kinds of questions in the first place.

I have heard it argued that people seek meaning in their lives when they feel that they are most insignificant; and, of course, if someone is looking for happiness outside of himself or herself, then disappointment is pretty much inevitable. I think that far more often than not these questions arise from the legitimate, however vague, suspicion that we are squandering something that is extraordinarily precious. We sense that we are somehow not quite awake to who we really are, and what we are doing here. In other words, I think that these questions actually represent our innate wisdom peeking through our own confusion.

The Buddha taught that all beings have this innate wisdom, or inherent potential, for full awakening. There is not one sentient being in the entire universe, from the lowest hell realms to the highest god realms, who does not have this potential. And this potential for Buddhahood, cultivated and brought to full fruition, is the most priceless possession in the whole universe. It simply has no comparison. Because it is the very nature of our mind—pure and stainless since beginningless time—buddhanature is not something that we have ever been without. Ironically, we look for it everywhere but right under our very noses. It is as if we have buried an enormous wealth and then in our confusion forgotten it. We build a shack over it and live in abject poverty. Our days are filled with the busyness of finding scraps to eat and rags to wear. Once in a while we have this faint remembrance, this vague sense that we are in truth extraordinarily well off. If we do not stick with this thought and clear away our confusion, however, our momentary insight quickly passes. If we would only stop looking everywhere else, and just tear down the shack and dig; we would discover what was ours all along. By coming to our senses we could then be of benefit to ourselves for the first time and of genuine benefit to others as well.

We have buried our own buddhanature. We have covered our innate wisdom and compassion under layer upon layer of habitual negative patterns and conflicting emotions, such as greed, anger, envy, grasping, hatred, possessiveness, and ill will. It is no particular surprise that we cannot think clearly. It is certainly no wonder that we are rarely of benefit to ourselves, let alone others. When our minds are so clouded, we are bound to experience continual frustration and dissatisfaction. We will also cause extraordinary unhappiness for others. So, if someone asked me how to find that which is most precious and meaningful in all of the universe, I would have to say, "Start digging!"

HON. CORINNE C. "LINDY" BOGGS

served as a member of the U.S. House of Representatives from 1973 to 1991, and is president of the Former Members of Congress. She is the author of Washington Through a Purple Veil: Memoirs of a Southern Lady. *Mrs. Boggs lives in New Orleans and Washington, D.C.*

I find God in the unfolding of the mysteries of the universe by the brave and knowledgeable astronauts and by the look of wonder in the eyes of my three-year-old great-granddaughter as she chases a butterfly. I find God in the flock of robins who unfailingly zoom down to the berries in my garden on their annual escape flight from the northern winters, and in my resident mockingbird who sits on the gnarled branch of an old tree and welcomes me home with his complete repertoire. I find God in all of the evidences of boundless hospitality provided by my children and their spouses and by my grandchildren in sharing their homes and their hearts with their friends and neighbors and with those who are troubled or displaced or ill. And I find God in an elderly neighbor searching through the crowded shelves of our corner grocery store for an expensive bottle of olive oil that his ill friend greatly enjoys but cannot afford.

I find God in the memory of my husband, Hale, and my daughter, Barbara, talented defenders of human rights, and of my last born, William, and of my parents and grandparents and aunts and uncles and cousins, all swirled together in the communion of saints. I find God in the love of holy tradition in my young friend, the wife of an admired rabbi, who revealed at their son's bar mitzvah that she had nervously anticipated her participation in the ceremony since the day of his birth.

I find God in the magnificent music of the gospel choirs of the predominately black church congregations in New Orleans, and in a young nun's crooning of the French lullaby *Frère Jacques* to an emaciated Cambodian baby amidst the sporadic shelling of a Thai refugee camp. I find God in the startling sight of the Washington Cathedral perched in strength and beauty atop Mt. Alto and curiously framed in the kitchen window of my Washington apartment. I find God in the old St. Louis Cathedral, my New Orleans parish church, an oasis of peace and tranquillity in the noisy, sometimes raucous, neighborhood. I find God through the example of Mary, the mother of Jesus, who opens my mind and soul to the inspiration of the Holy Spirit. Most especially, I find God in the Holy Eucharist, the ultimate act of unselfish love by his Divine Son.

ELIE WIESEL

is the Andrew W. Mellon Professor in the Humanities at Boston University. He has written widely on his experiences of the Holocaust, and is the author of over thirty books, including Night. *In 1986 he was awarded the Nobel Peace Prize.*

"How do I find God?" you ask. I do not know how, but I do know where—in my fellow man.

SOCORRO DURÁN,

sixty-six, of San Leandro, California, was born in Guadalajara, Mexico. At the age of twenty, she immigrated to the United States with her family. During that same year she met and married her husband, Manuel, also a recent immigrant from Mexico. Together they have raised three children: two boys and one girl. Today Socorro is very active in her Catholic parish. She coordinates outreach programs to the Latino community, works with people with AIDS, and helps immigrants from El Salvador resettle in the United States.

In my youth I was not very involved with the Church because at that time the Masses were still in Latin, and they bored me. But my mother was very Catholic, and made me go to Mass. The only memory I had was of priests who preached that everything was a sin, and that though you could confess your sins, you always remained stained by them. They taught me about a God who judges, rather than a God who loves.

I first came to know a simple, humble God, who loves us and wants to help us, when I got involved with Catholic Marriage Encounter and the Cursillo movement, that is, regular meetings of committed Catholics who wish to renew their faith. God, little by little, began to work in me. I formed a Cursillo community in Santa Felicitas, California, and another in San Leandro, where I am still active.

Soon I began to work with Latinos with AIDS, among whom were many homosexuals. One day a young man asked if I could show him the God of love, the one whom we speak of and preach about in Church. His own experience had been one of rejection by the Church for his being gay. Some in the Church had told him that he was going to be condemned. At that moment I didn't know what to say or how to respond to him. So I asked God for his help and he enlightened me. I said to the man, "For me, *you* are God, who suffers with AIDS. God is calling me to help you with love and tenderness. And you can see in me the God who loves you."

This was the first really strong experience of God in my life. God taught me through this man to accept gay people with respect and without judgment, and to accept my own son.

Two years ago I developed gout in my knee and I found I couldn't walk. I rebelled against God, telling him that I doubted that he was among us, because he had allowed me to get sick, despite the fact that since my husband's death I had dedicated my life to God. I challenged God to make himself present to me.

That day I had an appointment with my doctor. I was in so much pain that I couldn't even get into the car, and so I called the doctor to cancel my appointment. The nurse put me on hold and transferred me to another doctor. To my surprise, the doctor said that he would come to my house to see me. When he arrived I was lying down on my couch. He was a tall, thin, Jewish man who wore small glasses. He elevated my legs and I soon felt no pain at all. His hands were healing hands, filled with tenderness and love, and I felt through this doctor, the presence of Our Lord Jesus.

The most recent and profound experience of God came for me last year. A young gay, non-Catholic, English-speaking man named David developed cancer. David was a professor, a friend of my son. They had lived together for twelve years. He asked to live with us and die in our house. Together with my priest friends we used to speak with him about God. Whenever we asked if he wanted to pray with us, David always said yes. He never rebelled against God, and he never confronted God with his illness. He suffered his illness with resignation and he eventually accepted the anointing of the sick. He died praying with us.

At that same time, I had been ignoring my own health, and had not been feeling well. Finally, I went to see the doctor. The results of the tests revealed a tumor in one of my ovaries that weighed about thirty pounds. And at my age, there was a high probability of the tumor being cancerous. In that moment I remembered David, who had accepted his illness without rebelling against God. I felt that God was with me, that he had sent David to enable me to accept my own illness without rebelling against God. They finally had to operate on me. I put myself in God's hands and accepted his will without protesting. Thanks be to God I came out of the surgery all right. The tumor was not cancerous.

In conclusion, I can say that God is not only spirit; he is as human as we are. Each of us feels him and experiences him in a different way. He touches us and makes himself present among us, and in this way we know that God lives within each of us.

KENNETH L. WOODWARD

is a senior writer at Newsweek *magazine, where he has been religion editor since 1964, and has reported on intellectual and cultural issues from around the world. He is the winner of a National Magazine Award, and his articles and reviews have appeared in* The New York Times, Smithsonian, America, Commonweal, *and other national magazines. Mr. Woodward is also the author of* Making Saints, *a book about the Catholic Church's process of canonization. He and his wife, who live in Westchester County, New York, are the parents of three grown children.*

How, you ask me, can I find God?

"Who wants to know?" I must ask in return. The jungle out there is full of spiritual "seekers." So numerous are they that sociologists of religion now regard them as a distinct species. Hang out (as I have done) at the Sufi Bookstore in Manhattan and you'll soon be surrounded by seekers, flitting like butterflies from one tradition to another, sampling the nectar of now this, now that "mystical" tradition. It's Rumi one day, Ramakrishna the next, Teresa of Ávila and the Zohar on the weekend.

On my desk, in fact, is a letter from a reader who has discovered Kundalini Yoga and wonders if I have opened myself up to that "experience." No, I am about to write her, but I have it on the authority of Elisabeth Kübler-Ross, no less, that when the serpent energy coiled in the loins surges to the brain and bursts the lotus *chakra* (and it can happen when you least expect it), the experience feels like "ten thousand orgasms all at once." I already know what my correspondent's answer to me will be: "I'll have what she's having."

In my line of work, I am sometimes asked by those I interview to declare my own spiritual allegiance. Once, many years ago, under the insistent gaze of a Protestant evangelist, I told of how my Baptist father had been "converted" at age sixteen by Billy Sunday. Declared Jesus Christ to be his "personal" Lord and Savior, he did, on the spot, at a Sunday crusade in Youngstown, Ohio, in 1916. My story was true, but also a tease.

"And you," the evangelist prodded, hoping to discover whether the religion editor of *Newsweek* was saved or damned, "have you accepted Jesus like your father did?"

"Many times," I said. "With me, it's like sex: Once is not enough." Flip but true. In any case, I've never really wanted a "personal" savior anymore than I would use a personal tailor. I want the God off the rack, the God who manages to survive mangled parish liturgies, insipid hymns, sermons better left unpreached. The homely God of Here Comes Everybody, in the words of James Joyce.

For reasons too many to recite, a place like *Newsweek* does not attract many journalists who are also religious believers. More to the point, the culture of the mass media does not encourage examination of public issues from an angle informed by a religious perspective. In any case, those who do come here are, like salmon swimming upstream, in extended flight from whatever religious incubation they might have once received. Most have passed through corridors of higher education (at all the best places) where fundamental questions like "Is there a God?" do not get addressed, much less answered. Their certainties, such as they are, are of a secular sort.

So among my journalistic colleagues I've a history, a record of sorts, of being the go-to guy when someone in these precincts wants to talk about God. Just as the medicine editor, though not a physician, is often asked for free medical advice. Just as the justice editor is often put upon by colleagues with legal questions. It wasn't in the job description, but it goes with the territory. Become the religion editor and you're fair game for questions from the questing sort. Priests who teach in secular universities know exactly what I mean.

The questions I most often get are never as bare-faced as "How do I find God?" They are usually of the shyer variety. "What does the Catholic Church teach about this?" or (from lapsed Catholics) what does the Church say now about some half-remembered matter from their childhood instruction in the faith? Or, more boldly, "How can you still believe this?" What they are doing, of course, is sizing up this Woodward fellow. What's this resident alien, this *practicing* Catholic doing here?

So, yes, I am familiar with the question in its many disguises. And I have become aware, over the past three decades, that what I am is on the line. I am, in these instances, the Catholic Church, Christianity, or just belief in general. I am also, by nature, the adversative type. So, if my putative questioner meets me on *this* turf, he or she is likely to get an answer that finds fault with the questioner's assumptions, rather than one that says, "Look, here's how I find God."

How can we tell the seeker from the sought? Now *there's* a question. The God we seek is, most often, the God we want to find. But we who call ourselves Christians must conjure with a God who, if the Scriptures are to be believed, has first sought us. So how did God find this guy Woodward? No amount of circumambulating round this question, as Buddhists do in temples, will get me off the hook. I must speak plainly.

I think of life as a gift. I think of grace as a gift. What the gift of life begins, the gift of grace completes.

A bit more: I have become very aware that whatever I know of God has, through His grace, been given to me through others. Through family, yes, but above all through Catholic teachers, mentors from many quarters whom God has sent my way. What I am, essentially, for better (and occasionally for worse), is a creature of the Church. In a word, I have been *gifted* with and by the Church. And like gifts in native American culture, it is something that accrues in value as it is passed on. I have been gifted, too, in coming to know through my work others not of my own faith whose integrity, intellectual rigor, deep convictions (many of them far more open to God than I), passion, and (almost always) saving humor has sustained me in ways that I could not begin to recount. I have had the privilege of reporting about many of these people from time to time, knowing some quite well in person, others through their books. This is, alas, *not* humility speaking (I've rarely been accused of that) but statement of simple fact. The God who seeks me arrives through others. *Deo Gratias.*

What I *do* with those gifts is another matter. I'm not about to bare my soul in public. But a few things I can say that, if asked, might be of help to someone else.

Like a lot of other people who write, it is only through writing (especially books, but also letters and occasionally even journalism) that I learn how I feel about what it is I believe. Also, because a journalist inhabits a world of breaking news and endless chatter, of noise and buzz, I find it absolutely necessary to find time for silence, time to let the stream of words and images and concepts disappear, to get unwired. It's at times like these that I get an inkling of the unknown God who escapes all categories. In these moments, I get flashes of that emptiness that wears the face of God.

Sometimes, as an exercise, I imagine the Jesus I encounter in the Scriptures as a short and rather ugly fellow, and I go on to ask whether, had I lived when he was preaching and teaching, I would have followed him. Probably not, I fear. Even now, I find it hard to say with Jesus, "not mine but your will be done." I am dependent on the Holy Spirit, and on the prayers of those who pray for me.

Someday, God may really test me. Take away what He has so generously given. "My God, my God, why have you forsaken me?" Ask me then how I find God. Meanwhile, *Deo Gratias.*

JOSEPH LUMBARD

is an American who embraced Islam in his early twenties. "Because I believe in the truth of all revelation, I accepted Islamic revelation," he explains. "And since I perceive it as the last revelation, it seemed the logical choice in my life. Moreover, I felt I was not turning my back on Jesus because Jesus wants nothing more than for us to be close to God. For me, Islam was the way to do that."

Joseph, now twenty-six, received his master's in religious studies at The George Washington University, and is pursuing his doctorate in religious studies with a concentration in Islamic studies at Yale University in New Haven, Connecticut. He has published articles on Islamic mysticism, philosophy, and the environmental crisis in light of religious doctrine in Islamic Quarterly *and other scholarly journals.*

When the sincere seeker asks "How do I find God?" our answer should first focus on the necessity of prayer. There are many practices which should be a part of one's search for God, such as manifesting virtue, desisting from falsehood and reading religious texts, but prayer is the most direct and efficacious means of finding God, for in prayer one enters into dialogue with the Divine and exposes the illnesses and weaknesses of a soul suffering in its absence from God. The act of prayer is a way of admitting our complete and utter dependence upon God as well as our trust in His mercy, forgiveness, and guidance.

In Islam, the relationship between man and God is reflected in the position assumed for personal prayer. One rests upon the knees, cupping the hands, and delivers supplication to God. Being upon the knees is a sign of complete humility before God, while the cupping of the hands illustrates the readiness to accept all that comes from Him. But on a deeper level, the cupping of the hands illustrates our complete emptiness before the Divine, for as the Quran asserts, "God is the rich and ye are the poor." We are nothing without God and nothing comes to us but by His will. To turn to Him in prayer is to reflect this fundamental truth and thus the first and most valuable step in finding God, both for one who already follows a traditional religion and for one who seeks to do so.

In the modern world, those who want to find God can avail themselves of writings from any of the world's religions. This is a treasure which has never before been so readily accessible. It is, however, a double-edged sword. On the one hand, it can open the door to grace by offering many glimpses of the Divine. But on the other, it can lead to confusion by dragging the sincere seeker into a labyrinth of disputations to which there is no end. Each religion is efficacious in its own right and provides all that one needs in order to find and follow God. This is why the Quran commands Muslims to honor "the people of the book"—that is, those who adhere to the revelation which God has provided for them as a mercy and guidance.

From the Islamic perspective, each faith provides the devout worshiper all that is needed in order to live a life infused with the blessings of God and leading to paradise, however different their modes of expression may be. But, for this very reason, each path can only be followed according to its own dictates. There is no room for making one's own religion by mixing various practices and doctrines from different religions; to do so is the height of hubris, for it assumes that one knows better than God. To attempt to follow more than one path or to seek to create a new path is to follow no path. Because on the one hand, one cannot follow more than one path at a time. And on the other, religion is a gift of God, not a creation of man. The many similarities among the world's religions are due to their origin in the same source, while the many variations derive from the fact that they issue in different directions; just as the path up one side of a mountain will differ from that on the other, though they are upon the same mountain and lead to the same summit. To seek God with sincerity is to dedicate oneself to a single path, though this does not preclude one from admiring the beauty and respecting the truth of other religions.

Having discussed the centrality of prayer and the plurality of paths, I'll now turn to the specific nature of the quest for God in the Islamic context. In Islam, man is not conceived of as a fallen being in need of a "savior," but as a deiformic being who has forgotten God and is thus blind to his own true nature. The cure for the soul is therefore the remembrance of God, as such, the quintessence of Islam is the testimony of faith (*Shahadah*), "There is no god but God" (*La ilaha illa 'Llah*). To find God in the Islamic sense is to fully understand the implications of this sentence. This is achieved through the observance of three principles: *Iman* (faith), *Ihsan* (virtue), and *Islam* (submission). *Iman* is the fundamental acceptance of the Divine Unity. *Islam* is submission to all that this unity implies and thus to the will of God, while *Ihsan* is the means by which one deepens and perfects *Iman* and *Islam*. The prophet Muhammad has said "*Ihsan* is to adore God as though thou didst see Him, and if thou dost not see Him he nonetheless seeth thee." As regards *Islam*, *Ihsan* transforms the mere obedience to religious law (*Shari'ah*) into complete submission to the will of God. As regards *Iman*, it transforms one's belief in God into the certitude that He alone is Real.

For the religion of Islam, perfecting submission, faith, and sincerity is the way to find God. One who does this stills the confusion of the mind so that it is fit to meditate upon the Divine and polishes the mirror of the heart so that it is the undisturbed reflection of God. Such a person has wiped away the grime of forgetfulness to make way for the Presence of God. God, however, is never absent, the seeker has simply awakened to His eternal Presence.

MARK HELPRIN

is the author of the novels Winter's Tale, A Soldier of the Great War, *and* Memoir from Antproof Case, *as well as the short story collection* Ellis Island. *Mr. Helprin has been honored with the Jewish Book Award and the* Prix de Rome *for his work. In his letter, the novelist wrote: "Having created everything in six days, God is clearly fond of brevity, but having invented infinity, He is also tolerant of long-windedness. Choosing the former, I will respond with faith that if He wishes He will fill in whatever I leave out (this, the essence of poetry)."*

God is magnetized by the truth, and there you will find him, like the linnet dipping in the stream.

Jane Redmont,

"an American who was not born and raised in the U.S. and a Catholic who was not born and raised a Catholic," spent the first seventeen years of her life in France and became a Catholic while a master of divinity student at Harvard Divinity School in the mid seventies. She subsequently served as a minister in campus, parish, and urban settings.

A writer and theologian, she is the author of Generous Lives. American Catholic Women Today *and of a book on the experience of prayer in the contemporary world,* When in Doubt, Sing. *Ms. Redmont has also worked extensively with urban organizations addressing the causes and consequences of poverty in the Boston area. She now lives in Berkeley, California, where she is a Ph.D. student at the Graduate Theological Union and adjunct faculty member at the Jesuit School of Theology at Berkeley.*

Whoever you are, asking this question and reading these words, I want to honor your asking the question. It's a difficult and holy one, and the fact that you are asking it means that you have already, in some way, "found God." I write this in quotes because I am not sure one "finds God," and I am positive that no four-paragraph answer will give you magic wings to fly in that direction. Nevertheless: a few thoughts for you, with my deepest respect, in what will often feel more like slogging through the mud than being carried on angels' wings.

My answer is necessarily colored by my experience as a Catholic Christian, though I do not for one minute believe that this path is the only one to God, not even the best. Only God knows the answer to this mystery, and only you can determine, with much thought, prayer, discernment, trial and error, and help from wise companions, what tradition, what path, what practice will be your way to God—or your way to let God come to you.

Hearing your questions as I do, as a Christian, I keep hearing Jesus' words to his would-be disciples, who asked him, "Where do you live?" Their question contained others: How do we find you and what you stand for? For what and for whom do you live and die? Jesus answered: "Come and see." I say to you: "Go and see." Don't think too much about "finding God." Do something, and the finding will follow. I once preached a homily about how one finds hope by committing acts of hope. It may be the same with faith. Start doing it. Any part of it. Prayer, care of the poor, actions on behalf of justice, deep wrestling with and reading of good theological texts, singing gospel hymns or the Fauré *Requiem*, whatever is congenial to you and to your life at present.

And do it on two levels. Of course find what speaks to your deepest heart. Go to that intimate place where you are infinitely sad, or ecstatic, or creative or talented, or bereft or deeply engaged, and there you will find God, if you enter into that place and ask what it means for you and for the world that you are there. This will require of you both ruthless honesty and tenderness with yourself.

The second level may be even more important because you have asked "How do *I* find God?" Go find yourself a "we." A community, any community. A Christian community, if the path into which you are drawn or were born is Christian; a Jewish one, if you are a Jew by birth or by choice, a Muslim one if that is your path. (I would say the same for the great religious paths that do not have a God, such as Buddhism—where one "takes refuge in the Buddha, the *dharma*, and the *sangha*," the community.) Find yourself a community of practice and faith—one that meets your standards of intellectual honesty, lack of hypocrisy, sincere concern for others, non-coercive welcome of the stranger.

If the community is Christian, it might be a parish; it might also be a prayer group or a Catholic Worker House, or a Bible study group, or a Women-Church liturgical gathering, or a team that cares and prays for people with AIDS, or an adult education class with some soul and some teeth. You may have to look around, and you may have to try a few different groups. Give them a chance. "Come and see." Then stay for a while. See what happens. "Finding God" often happens in the midst of a "we." That's why so many of those biblical stories about the Holy Spirit happen to groups.

I know. Groups are difficult. Common life is messy. Institutional religion may have wounded you—hence my listing of several forms of community, in the hope that you will find one as a gateway into the common life which is faith. God alone can answer the lonely yearning inside that heart of yours, which is like no other heart. But God without the "we" experience is not the God of whom the Jewish and Christian Scriptures speak. God is involved in history—in *our* history. In history, past and present (and, I hope, future), you will find God. I pray that you will meet companions along the way. In their friendship, you will find God, and God will find you.

RABBI STACY LAVESON

decided to become a rabbi shortly after moving to Salt Lake City, Utah, at the age of twelve. After graduating from Brandeis University with a degree in sociology and attending the Hebrew University in Jerusalem, Stacy entered rabbinical school at the Hebrew Union College-Jewish Institute of Religion. She studied in Israel, Los Angeles, and New York, before being ordained in 1993. Presently she is a rabbi at Congregation Rodef Sholom in San Rafael, California. "Being a rabbi allows me to share holy moments with people, some of their most intimate moments," she says, "and there's nothing better than that."

Her professional interests include interfaith and youth work, spirituality and worship, and issues of death and dying. Personally, Rabbi Laveson, who is thirty-three, enjoys singing, dancing, hiking, cooking, traveling, and, as she says, "sitting on my deck watching the fog."

I recently had lunch with a friend of mine. After we finished our sushi, shared the latest details of our lives, and paid the bill, my friend looked at me oddly and commented, "You really have tremendous faith in God." "I do," I responded, "when I remember to." Our lunch was one of those times when I "remembered" God, when God's compassion helped to ease my friend's burdens, when God's wisdom seemed to justify my personal challenges, and when God's presence clarified the murky ambiguity of both our lives. It is at such instances when I experience the world with distinct clarity, when everything makes sense, because I view everything as pertaining to God, the ultimate Creator and Sustainer.

There are times, however, when I "forget" to believe in God. Rather than a conscious or voluntary act, forgetting seems to be something that just happens to me. After moments, days, and occasionally even weeks when God's presence pervades me and the world around me, I suddenly realize that it is gone, that my awareness of God has left me without my notice. While I know intellectually that God exists, my faith in God has left me, and I am alone. My world seems dimmer, my challenges more burdensome, my path steeper and more of a struggle to climb. I have lost that powerful essence which enables me to transcend the mundane, which brings unity to my life, and which illuminates my world.

Yet while "forgetting" is not a conscious act, "remembering" is. Only when I look for evidence of God's presence, only when I recognize that God is part of every relationship I have, every bite of food I eat, and every drop of rain that falls from the sky, will my intellectual knowledge of God be replaced by an intimate awareness of God. For when I am face to face with God, I cannot help but have faith in God. For me, it is Jewish rituals, prayer, and *mitzvot* (God's commandments and good deeds) that most ably place me and my life in the context of the Divine. They help me to "remember" my faith in God, and they place me face to face with God's radiant light.

The Baal Shem Tov, the founder of Hasidism, explained that when God finished creating the heavens and the earth, God returned to heaven. Overflowing with joy, God celebrated, taking radiant sparks of light, throwing them up into the air, and watching them fall to the earth. For a moment, the earth radiated with glorious light as the sparks of God poured down from heaven. As they landed, however, the sparks became imbedded in everything they touched. Eventually, the earth darkened, the divine sparks smoldering deep within every rock, and tree, and within every human heart as well. Realizing that we could no longer see the bright sparks, God gave us tools with which to uncover them, thereby rekindling our relationship with God and once again illuminating our world.

It is with the aid of these tools, rituals, *mitzvot*, and prayer, that I am able to push back the gray fog that hides the sparks of divinity which hover just below the surface. For example, I usually recite a blessing, the *motzi*, before I eat. When I recite this ten-word, ancient formula, eating is transformed into an encounter with God. No longer is a muffin just a muffin, no longer is a sandwich two pieces of bread with something in between. Rather, eating becomes an encounter with God because the blessing reminds me that my food did not come from my refrigerator nor from my grocery store. Rather, it came to me via the rain, the sun, the people who tilled the soil and harvested the land and worked in the store which sold the food. When I recite the blessing, I become part of an awesome chain of people, events, and places which created my food. Once again, I can see the spark in all of these things, in all of these people.

I believe that God exists not only in nature and all that it produces but also in relationship with other people and within ourselves as well. In Genesis we read that we were each created in the image of God. When we are true and kind to ourselves, we fan the flame of divinity within us. When we have loving, honest, respectful relationships with other people, we nourish the essence of God in them. And when we treat strangers as we would like to be treated ourselves, we honor the divine Presence in them as well. We essentially release the sparks previously hidden within the human heart, so often hardened by a life lived in darkness. The 613 *mitzvot*, or commandments, in the Torah help us to relate to others and ourselves in an ethical, compassionate, and holy way. They are our tools for uncovering the godliness and accentuating the divine image in every human being.

Yet despite these potent tools that draw our attention to God and which invite God into our relationship with others and the world, there are still times when I cannot feel God's presence. I know there is something beautiful, awesome, and comforting out there, but I can't see it or experience it, for I am lost in a thick, gray fog that obscures the wonder of God from me. I am left longing for the clarity that exists beneath the fog, yearning for God's closeness.

I have come to understand, however, that the fog itself is an essential part of my relationship with God, that patient periods of ambiguity, doubt, and distance will eventually lead me to greater clarity and a deeper connection. As a Jew, I am also called *b'nai Yisrael*, a child of God. *Yisrael*, or Israel, literally meaning one who struggles with God. That struggle with God occurs amidst the fog. When I muddle through the fog long enough, grappling to find evidence of God, always a bright light eventually peers through the darkness leading me to more of God's divine sparks.

When I first moved to the San Francisco area from New York three years ago, a friend of mine brought me to what she claimed was the most beautiful spot in the Bay Area. When we arrived at the top of a jagged bluff overlooking the Golden Gate Bridge, my friend took a deep breath and beamed with pride and serenity. I, on the other hand, took a shallow, frustrated breath, and quickly announced that I had to get back into the car. I felt lost as I stood out in the cold, wet winds overlooking gray layers of fog. This was simply not my idea of beauty, nor did this fit my image of a hot, summer afternoon! As we hastily made our way back to the car my friend predicted that I'd get used to foggy summer days and that I would probably even learn to like the fog. "I sincerely doubt that," I replied.

Today, as I reflect upon that day, I can still vividly recall how alienated from my surroundings I felt, how alone, how disconnected. It was as if there was something wonderful surrounding me and I couldn't see it or understand it or experience it. In the three years I have lived in the San Francisco area, however, I have come to appreciate, even cherish the fog. I now make a practice of sitting on my deck each morning, sipping my tea, and watching the fog. A sense of calm and tranquility descends upon me as I focus on the still, gray strands of fog that rest in the valley below my home.

At times, it is enough for me to see only the fog. Perhaps the same is true of the fog that descends upon me when God's presence leaves me. For during those times, I must have faith that God's presence, like the trees and houses below the fog, still fills the world, illuminating every human heart, every action, and every bit of creation with God's wonder, majesty, and sanctity.

Tino Quiles,

twenty-one, recently turned away from his affiliation with the Latin King gang in Milwaukee, Wisconsin. In his heyday, Tino kept an arsenal of guns under his waterbed and proudly displayed his Latin King tattoos. Today, Tino is an evangelical Christian who walks the street with other friends helping other gang members come to know God. A black leopard tattoo now camouflages his old gang symbols, and as he says, "Instead of packing guns we're packing Bibles."

Through Homeboyz Graphics, an organization that employs former gang members, Tino designs colorful T-shirts depicting two roads for Latino youths: gangs, drugs, prison, and death on one side, and pride in Hispanic culture, faith in God, jobs, and new life on the other. He also designs computer web sites for Homeboyz' web site development training business, and hopes one day to manage his own web site firm. From a very young age, Tino has enjoyed writing poetry, and his response is entitled Dying to Old Life.

There is death all around,
Death in the streets.
There is death from drugs,
Death from guns.
There is death from drinking.

Slowly sinking.
I see Death in vacant lots.
I see the Devil making plots,
Attacking us in our weak spots.
There is death in changing seasons,
Just so many reasons.

But unless the seed falls to the ground
And is buried, it cannot bear fruit.
Only if we die to our old self,
Through you, Lord,
Will we afford True Life.
There is death all around me,
Death in Thee.

STANLEY HAUERWAS,

a noted ethicist, is well known for his work in bringing concepts like character, narrative, and community into the sphere of ethical reflection. He is the author of numerous books, including A Community of Character: Toward a Constructive Christian Ethic *and* The Peaceable Kingdom: A Primer in Christian Ethics. *Professor Hauerwas is the Gilbert T. Rowe Professor of Theological Ethics at the Divinity School of Duke University, in Durham, North Carolina.*

What do you do when someone asks you a question you do not like? The answer to the question "How can I find God?" invites the presumption that we know a kind of God for which we are looking. In contrast, those who have preceded us in the Christian faith usually put the matter as: "What do I do now that God has found me?" For that is the kind of God Christians believe has refused to abandon God's good creation, which is revealed through the people of Israel and the life, death, and Resurrection of Jesus of Nazareth. Such a God is not easily found because we cannot find that which is as near to us as our next breath and as far from us as the silence that surrounds all language.

Yet I fear that such a response might "put off" those who ask the question "How can I find God?" For that can be an important and powerful question. The best way to discover that God has already discovered them through the asking of the question is to go to a person who is an adept practitioner of the Christian faith. That means one must apprentice oneself to someone who has learned to pray. The way one locates such a person is by going to church. So nothing can be more important than simply turning up and placing oneself amidst people who are praying to and praising the One known as Father, Son, and Holy Spirit.

REV. CANON JOHN ANDREW, O.B.E., D.D.,

is rector of Saint Thomas Episcopal Church on Fifth Avenue in New York City, where he has served since 1972. Father Andrew was educated in England at Keble College, Oxford, and at Cuddesdon Theological College. He served in the Royal Air Force from 1949 to 1951. Prior to his appointment at Saint Thomas, Father Andrew served as chaplain to the archbishop of York and the archbishop of Canterbury. In these positions he preached extensively throughout the United States, Canada, Europe, and the United Kingdom and frequently before the British Royal Family. In 1996 he was made an officer of the Order of the British Empire at Buckingham Palace.

Father Andrew is the author of Nothing Cheap And Much That Is Cheerful *and* My Heart Is Ready: Feasts and Fasts on Fifth Avenue.

People will insist on the needle-in-the-haystack principle when the whole discussion of getting into touch with God, or finding God, is begun. God plays hard to find, they complain. I suspect that God only plays hard to find with people who are convinced that they have guessed his personality already and have a picture of God that suits them, because they cannot possibly entertain a notion of the "Other" in their reckoning. So his personality, his "reachableness" eludes them. He is not at home. The chances are that they are knocking on the door of the wrong house. He is not available to the aggrieved, the angry, the self-justificatory, or the vindictive, not because he removes himself from availability but because these postures face the wrong direction: away from him. You see this in the psalms, God berated querulously for not being awake and alert to human need, slow to take up the cudgels for the worthy and the right, failing to punish the evildoer. We are experts at making God in our own image. But he remains as such an illusory God. It is a difficult exercise to empty oneself of projection and to wake contentedly empty-handed, for him to fill. But I am convinced that the only expectation we can rightly claim is that he *will* manifest himself and has in fact already done so: in a human frame, in Christ his Son, because love is self-declaratory; it cannot remain content *not* to move out in a gesture of embrace. And Christ has embraced us both in our total humanity and in being willing to give us everything of himself.

So, mysteriously and curiously, it is we who have been found, for all initiative to discover and embrace is part of the Divine *esse*.

It is true that God hides himself, not to be unfindable but in order to avoid being misunderstood. Holy people have spent their lives content with the knowledge that since love seems to be his personal description and activity, where there is love there is God: *Ubi est amor, ibi Deus.* Certainly the fact of Christ living among us would seem to support their acceptance of this belief.

There is a stack of obstacles to getting through to God that can prove insurmountable by people. I am not sure that God erects them. They are what we can describe as the Unanswerable Questions. I write a few weeks after the massacre of sixteen five-year-olds at play in a school gymnasium in Dunblane, Scotland. Why, if God is a god of love, if he is love, does this have to happen? Of all God's human creatures, aren't five-year-olds perhaps the crown of his human creation for beauty, for innocence, for curiosity, for energy, for creativity, for openness to giving and receiving love, for capacity to wonder and ask the profoundest questions, for eye-sparkle and for our enchantment and fascination? How *could* a god who wants to declare himself simply withdraw some sort of restraint upon a person with murder on his mind? The silent *emptiness* after that terrible moment, the vacuum of awareness of God's presence in that quiet Scotland town as people gazed on a pile of lifeless dolls strewn over one another screamed louder than that murderous gunfire.

Where can God be in all of this, if there is a God?

Some years ago, I experienced a mugging that nearly killed me. My skull was smashed in and my right forearm destroyed. (All now fully restored by the skills of two inspired young geniuses of surgeons.) In my hours of inactivity in the hospital bed, lying comfortably and without pain, I very clearly felt that God was *inside* the experience, going through it with me, and making his presence very real to me. The discovery of his close reality surprised me, and I welcomed it wonderingly..."surely the Lord was in this place, and I knew it not..."

The notion of a suffering God helping to absorb some of the pain and sense of violation isn't an immediately obvious concept to those who are puzzled at an absence of God.

To them, as to all who complain that God has somehow removed himself from their ability to reach him, I am always tempted to ask, "Who moved?"

DAVID PLANTE,

a novelist and essayist, was born to parents of French-Canadian descent in Providence, Rhode Island. The second youngest of seven brothers, he was educated at Catholic schools, including La Salle Academy and Boston College. The most widely known of his novels are the Francoeur trilogy— The Foreigner, The Catholic, *and* The Native—and The Family, *which was nominated for the National Book Award in 1978. Mr. Plante also writes nonfiction, primarily for* The New Yorker, *which has published many of his profiles. He has lived in London for most of the past thirty years, but also in Belgium, Italy, and Russia, where he was the first Westerner to lecture at the Gorky Institute of Literature.*

I stopped believing in God at the age of nineteen, in 1959, on a tower overlooking the city of Copenhagen. The moment in which it occurred to me that God did not exist—occurring in much the same way grace is meant to occur: with a sense of sudden freedom—was a moment of great reassurance and joy.

Now, almost forty years later, I begin to discern in the shadows of the religious devotion of my youth—because I was, until nineteen, a deeply devout young man—the outline of a God who existed within the God I ceased to believe in. Whereas I have for years thought that the God of my youth was one God and entirely to be rejected in my realization that God did not exist, I begin to see that in my devotion I believed in two Gods, one within the other. I begin to recognize that in denying the existence of the outer God—the God of Will, dogma, rectitude, and condemnation—I was also denying the existence of the inner God, who was altogether different.

Who was this inner God? To be able to give Him presence would require me to describe my parish, a small Franco-American parish in Providence, Rhode Island, which consisted of French Canadians whose parents and grandparents had come down from Canada at the turn of the century to work in the New England textile mills, whose parents and grandparents and great and great-great grandparents had lived in the great forests of Canada for hundreds of years and intermarried with the Indians and evolved a religion which, nominally Catholic, was as unique to them as a North American bird found nowhere else in the world but in their forests. Within the God of Will, dogma, rectitude and condemnations was a God for people who had learned that their wills did not count for much because they were essentially helpless in this world—the God for people who knew that the doctor would not get through the snow storm to save the dying mother, that the crop would fail, that the bank would foreclose.

He, too, was helpless. If He could have done something, could have saved one baby, in all the history of humankind, from suffering, and didn't, He was not God. The outer God of Will, dogma, rectitude, and condemnation told us He could have done something, but He also told us that, to give us the freedom of our wills (which wills were in fact not free, but, for their salvation, had to abide obediently by His Will), He would do nothing. The inner God never claimed He could do anything, but, in His own helplessness, He understood the weakness of our wills and our helplessness and grieved for us. He grieved for us, and in His grief for us He loved us, for our helplessness. For this we loved Him at moments of great, soul-opening joy and reassurance when in our helplessness we were too weak to love—that is, to obey—the outer God, our love for whom—that is, our obedience to whom—closed our souls. And in our love for the inner God, He made us understand that His longing for us to love one another in our loving Him was His greatest longing.

I do not believe in this God of my shadowed youth, but I often pray to Him. And perhaps it is in praying to a God one does not believe in that one finds Him.

Sister Joan Chittister, O.S.B.,

is an author and lecturer on topics of spirituality, religious life, peacemaking, and social justice. Currently she is executive director of Benetvision, a resource and research center for contemporary spirituality. Sister Joan, a member of the Benedictine Sisters of Erie, is also past president of the Leadership Conference of Women Religious.

She is author of several books, including The Fire in These Ashes: A Spirituality of Contemporary Religious Life, In a High Spiritual Season, *and* Wisdom Distilled from the Daily: Living the Rule of St. Benedict Today, *as well as numerous articles on religious life, spirituality, and other contemporary issues. Sister Joan holds a doctorate in speech communications theory and has taught at all educational levels. She lives with her Benedictine community in Erie, Pennsylvania.*

The Sufi tell stories that say all I think I'll ever know about finding God.

The first story is a disarming and compelling one. It is also, I think, a troublesome one, a fascinating one, a chastening one: "Help us to find God," the seeker begged the Elder. "No one can help you there," the Elder answered. "But why not?" the seeker insisted. "For the same reason that no one can help a fish to find the ocean." The answer is clear: There is no one who can help us find what we already have.

The second story is even more challenging. "Once upon a time," the Sufi say, "a seeker ran through the streets shouting over and over again, *We must put God into our lives. We must put God into our lives.*" "Ah, poor soul," an Elder smiled wanly. "If only we realized the truth: God is always in our lives. The spiritual task is simply to recognize that."

As a Benedictine, a disciple of an order historically devoted to the Sacrament of the Ordinary, I know how disappointing, how exhilarating that kind of advice can be. The neophyte seeks to pass the test of spiritual heroics; the wise seek to accomplish only the testimony of integrity. The young think the task is to buy God by their good efforts; the insightful know that the task is to want God beyond the lure of lesser ends, including even the trappings of spirituality.

For my own part, I entered religious life intent on being spiritually intrepid. I wanted something far more romantic than the Sacrament of the Ordinary. I expected to find formulas tried and true, ideas that were esoteric, a life that was mystical, a regimen that was at least duly demanding, if not momentously ascetic. What I found were spiritual manuals that were convoluted and academic, at best, and a community that was simple and centered in God always. The writers had missed the mark; the women were living the life. It was very disappointing. And it was very right.

God is not in the whirlwind, not in blustering and show, Scripture teaches us. God is in the breeze, in the very atmosphere around us, in the little things that shape our lives. God is in the contradictions that assail us, in the circumstances that challenge us, in the attitudes that impel us, in the motives that drive us, in the life goals that demonstrate our real aspirations, in the burdens that wear us down, in the actions that give witness to the values in our hearts. God is in the stuff of life, not in the airy-fairy of fertile imaginations bent on the pursuit of the preternatural. God is where we are, including in the very weaknesses that vie for our souls.

Benedictine spirituality attends to those things, not to tricks and trials designed to make spiritual athletes out of spiritual weaklings. Finding God depends on finding what determines our own lives and realizing in them the power and transcendence of what is God.

I learned from holy women before me that finding God depends on four things: a conscious awareness of the presence of God, the sacralization of life, an attunement to the Holy Spirit, and a sense of place in the universe.

A conscious awareness of the presence of God requires the development of a sincere and serious prayer life that is more reflective, thoughtful, and contemplative than it is mere rote and ritual. "Going to church" is not a substitute for putting myself in the presence of God. Turning our minds and hearts over to the God of the universe puts us in the place of That Which we seek. The purpose of prayer is not to make God conscious of us; it is to make us conscious of God. It is to attend to the God in whom we live and whose presence we either ignore or expect to find somewhere else.

The sacralization of life requires us, in the words of Benedict of Nursia's fifteen-century-old *Rule*, to "treat all things as vessels of the altar"—to hold every isolated thing in high regard whatever their use, to treat them gently, to take care of them well whatever their age. It leads us to become part of the holiness of the universe by recognizing each and every element of it as a spark of the Divine. It nurtures in us that sense of the sacred in all things so that the presence of God becomes a fact of life, not a myth to be fabricated. It leads us to save and care and preserve and respect the goods of material creation so that we can come to respect the spiritual energy that underlies each of them. It is learning to live in sacred space again so that we can be surprised by God. We are part of a holy universe, not its creators and not its rulers. God has done the creating, God does the judging, and God waits for us to realize that.

An attunement to the Holy Spirit enables us to hear the Word of God in those around us and in the circumstances of our lives—in our culture, in our sexuality, and in the racial makeup that is the raw material of our being. It lies in bringing each of those things to fulfillment—whatever the obstacles to each. Everything we are, everything that is said to us, everything that happens to us is some kind of call from God. In fact, everything that happens is God's call to us either to accept what we should not change or to change what we should not accept so that the Presence of God can flourish where we are. Until we learn to listen to these manifestations of divine presence all around us in life, we need not expect visions.

A sense of our place in the universe is what Chapter Seven of the *Rule of Benedict* calls "The Twelve Degrees of Humility." In one of the earliest pieces of Western spiritual literature, Benedict is very clear that the beginning of a spiritual life depends on the realization that we live in the womb of God, that we need to admit our struggles, that we need to accept the inconsequential circumstances of life with equanimity, and that we need to cultivate, to tread lightly through the universe and to deal tenderly with both ourselves and others.

Finding God is a matter of seeing God where God is, of seeing the God who is in us to sustain us, around us to touch us, before us to beckon us onward in life. Finding God is a matter, not of learning to become something we are not but of learning to see what we already know, to touch what we already contain, to recognize what we already have. Finding God is a matter of living every minute of life to its ultimate. "Oh, wonder of wonders," the Zen teacher teaches. "I chop wood. I draw water from the well." Finding God has little to do with church and more to do with becoming the best of everything we are every moment we breathe.

God is not a mystery to be sought in strange places and arcane ways. God is a mystery to be discovered within us and around us. And savored.

Mary Armitage,

as a young woman during the Second World War, served in the Aviation personnel department of the U.S. Marine Corps, working in the Marine Air Infantry school at Quantico, Virginia, from 1943 to 1945. Over the next few decades Mrs. Armitage raised twelve children with her husband, Henry, a local physician, at their home in North Andover, Massachusetts.

Just recently, after a long illness, Henry passed away. Today, Mrs. Armitage is a staff member of the Immigrant City Archives of the city of Lawrence, Massachusetts, where she works compiling oral histories. She is a member of the Betsy Ross/Samuel Adams chapter of the Daughters of the American Revolution and also enjoys oil painting, writing, and spending time with her children and her grandchildren. She is also a member of the Third Order Franciscans, a Catholic lay group. "Oh, but I'm a very poor member!" she says.

Perhaps it is expected that I will tell you that you will find Him whom angels fear and adore in written words and rituals, or in some inner part of yourself. But how can I tell you this when He who is everywhere eludes my own faithful mind and heart? Instead, I can merely suggest that you try to recognize His signs as you pass through life.

When in the East there is a lemon sky we do not have to see

the sun to know that dawn is near. Nor when apricot sunset silhouettes a naked tree we do have to see the volcano to know that its ash is medium for tone and hue. Nor when peepers peep do we have to see small frogs to know that spring's magic has begun. And when "bleak mid-winter" with its cruel brilliance strengthens us for trials to come, the geometry of chill and fragile flake tells us with tender mercy of Other Power and might.

Maybe I'm supposed to say that in the twelve that I have borne, two daughters and ten sons, that I have found the pulse of God and therefore can pass that knowledge on to you. But that would not be true. Actually, I sense through them the truth of exile; which is perhaps a gift in this world of instant Shangri-las and Utopias.

So the most I can say to you is see, really see, His Signs. It will give you sustenance for your search. And maybe once or twice in time there will come an unmistakable and precious moment when He will reveal himself to you. Then, with gentle grace and knowing heart, He will let you think that you have discovered Him, and He will lead you where He will.

Albert White Hat

*(*Natan Tokahe, *or, The First One to Charge) is a member of the Rosebud tribe of the Lakota nation. His mother was born in Crow Indian Territory, where her father, Chief Hollow Horn Bear, had traveled to forge a peace with the Lakota's traditional enemies. Since the mid seventies Mr. White Hat has taught oral history and the Lakota language in the Lakota Studies department of Sinte Gleska University in Mission, South Dakota. He has served on a number of tribal councils and also acted as the Lakota translator for the film* Dances with Wolves. *Currently, he is writing a Lakota language textbook.*

It was perhaps not surprising that given his background, Mr. White Hat preferred to answer the question orally, so his response takes the form of our conversation.

In its simplest form the question is: If someone were to ask you, "How can I find God?" what would you tell them?

You know, I'm fifty-seven years old now and I hadn't thought about this issue until about thirty years ago. The thing that I've learned is first to try to give people my idea of the different religions and explain what I know about them. Then I suggest that they question each one and go with the one that they're comfortable with. And I also present my own philosophy as another option. But I try to stress that nobody should tell you that this is God.

What would you tell someone about your own tradition? If someone asked you, "Where do I start?"

I would tell them to learn all about relationships and the idea of relatives. Our philosophy is based on relationship.

Can you explain that?

We come from one Source and that Source created everything by draining its blood to create. So, each time creation came in, its energy was growing weaker and weaker, and its spirit was draining out. When creation was completed, it completely dried up and scattered all over the world.

The story means that all creation is God—that the idea of God is not separate from creation. And that as creation comes through, each creation demonstrates a different behavior, some good behavior and some negative. This indicates that every creation has good and evil in it. The idea of God and Satan—that's not the way we look at it. We see every creation as having the concept of Satan in it and the concept of God in it, and it's up to the individual to develop one or the other. Whichever one you develop, that's what you'll find in creation.

How would someone move closer to creation?

It's how you relate to creation and how you deal with human relations. You can associate with the good or the evil. They're both in existence today. The energy of the negative force comes from a living being—you have that in you and you can draw it out of you. Goodness is in every creation, too. And if you practice goodness, you will draw that goodness out of creation.

Why does the tradition emphasize relatives and family?

Well, supposedly you're on good terms with your relatives—your brothers, sisters, mother, father, those kinds of relationships—and this is what you practice with creation. Prayer, as I understand it, is talking to God. But in Christianity, for example, this doesn't mean that you talk to relatives. When you pray you talk to God—you don't talk to your relatives. You talk *above* them.

And in your tradition?

You talk to creation, you talk to your relatives, you talk to your sister, you talk to your brother. The idea of "prayer" today is that it puts you above everything. It's just a little thing, but a little thing like this can take that respect away from creation.

Do people ask you questions like this?

Oh, all the time! Particularly in the last twenty years. People are seeking spirituality.

In my tribe, at least, we all approach the philosophy differently. Sometimes, for example, someone will come back from the city and say, "I want to learn about the Sun Dance." And I usually tell them to make time for it, to take at least three to four years to study it. Go to every Sun Dance you can. Get to know the leaders and get to know the people. Especially the leaders—because they will usually work with you. Get to know them and their families, because when you dance you'll have to work with them and depend on them. And after you've met all these leaders, then think about it, and go to the one you're most comfortable with.

I say that if you're relaxed and you make an appeal and ask for help it will all come out honestly. Our philosophy really dictates responsibility. When these young people research and study they come to a point where they have to make decisions and be responsible for it.

But I don't tell people how to pray and do the spiritual life. You teach, and it's their decision.

DAVID S. BENNETT, JR.,

was inducted into the Army Air Force in July 1943, at the age of eighteen, three weeks after graduating from high school. He flew fifty combat missions over Europe as a ball-turret gunner in a B-24 Liberator before completing his tour of duty in the Second World War. His plane, named "Dopey" (after one of the Seven Dwarves), crashed seven times. "And each time I walked away from it," he said.

After the war Dave began a career in banking and served as an officer and director of several savings and loan associations in Philadelphia. Throughout his adult life he has been active as a ruling elder, trustee, deacon, and Sunday School teacher in the Presbyterian church. He lives with his wife of forty-three years, June, in Bryn Mawr, Pennsylvania, and has two daughters and four grandchildren.

Though I am neither a theology scholar nor very profound, maybe the experiences that I share could be the light you need to start you on the road to finding God. Acceptance did not come to me like a lightning bolt; it was a long process over many years, and still continues.

As a lad of seven, and on, I saw the love of God through my mother and her dedication to church and family. I knew about God in my youth, having been sent to Sunday School, but at that time I really couldn't say that I had "found" him. Then, at the young age of eighteen, I served in the Army Air Force and flew fifty combat missions over Europe. After two of us—myself and the tail gunner—had completed our missions, the rest of my crew flew two final missions over the Ploesti oil fields in Rumania. The second time out, six of my crew were lost, two were captured.

Before I left for the war, my mother gave me a pocket Bible with a metal cover, which I carried in my chest pocket. The word of God and the cover served me well.

It was not the Bible alone, but my mother's love that guided me, helping me to avoid the temptations that were readily available. If tempted I used to say, "What would Mother think?" My mother's love was God's love within her, and God's love shined through her.

We can't see God—or can we? I think we can, in countless ways. Most especially, God's love shines in the lives of others who we meet along the way. When we love others it provides us light to remove the barrier of darkness that prevents us from finding him. If you will seek God, you will find him if you search after him with all your heart and soul.

CATHERINE MOWRY LACUGNA

is the Dreux Professor of Theology at the University of Notre Dame. Professor LaCugna has also taught at Fordham University, Vassar College, and Boston College. In addition to articles in numerous theological journals, she is the author of God for Us: The Trinity and Christian Life *and editor of* Freeing Theology: The Essentials of Theology in Feminist Perspective.

One "finds" God because one is already found by God. Anything we would find on our own would not be GOD. If we think that by our own efforts, or our own ideas, we have found GOD, we may have "found" just a product of our own imaginations, or needs, or wishful thinking. But it might be difficult to tell the difference between the true, living God, and the God whom we have devised for ourselves, a God enshrined in expected religious symbols and ritual gestures. God who dwells in light inaccessible exceeds every concept and image we have of God; else, God would not be GOD. The Carmelite Ruth Burrows puts it this way: "We want our own version of [God], one we can, so to speak, carry around in our pockets rather as some superstitious people carry around a charm. We can hold endless, loving conversations with this one, feel we have an intimate understanding with him, we can tell him our troubles, ask for his approbation and admiration, consult him about all our affairs and decisions and get the answer we want, and this god of ours has almost nothing to do with God." The only sure path to finding the true living God is to be rid of all impediments and sin—to this end there is no alternative but discipline, ascesis, and above all, ceaseless prayer.

One well-recognized way to guard against idolatry is known as the *via negativa*, the path through denial and darkness that leads us toward the effulgent life of the true, living God. The whole of the Christian tradition is full of examples and endorsements of the *via negativa*. At the same time, Gregory of Nyssa, Anselm, Catherine of Siena, Teresa of Ávila, and other great theologians and mystics through the ages have balanced the perspective by the "positive way," which affirms the very real knowledge of God to be found in creation/nature, in the desires of the human heart, and in the capacity of human beings for deep communion with other persons and with all creatures. Indeed, we are made to know and love God through love of others, love of self, love of all creatures. We discover the ever-present God in our own goodness, creativity and capacity for self-transcendence. God desires nothing more than to be known and loved by us, to be in eternal communion with us—which is why we are indeed already found by the true, living God.

Cardinal Joseph Bernardin

served for forty-four years as a priest and thirty as a bishop before his death from cancer in 1996. In his role as archbishop of Chicago, he helped to influence this country's thinking on issues as diverse as nuclear disarmament, abortion, euthanasia, and care for the marginalized, as well as more specifically religious issues, such as the role of women in the modern Church. In 1996 he received the Medal of Freedom, the nation's highest civilian honor, from President Bill Clinton.

His posthumous book, The Gift of Peace, *which detailed in moving terms his battle with cancer, his trust in God, and his acceptance of death, became a national bestseller in 1997. Cardinal Bernardin wrote the essay here a few months before it was discovered that his cancer had recurred.*

How can I find God? The question is so simple—so profound! Allow me to answer it by reflecting on my own journey of faith and how I came to find God.

My life is not so very different from your own. My specific responsibilities as a pastor may vary from yours, but I have to face the same basic human issues that you do. I get caught up in the maelstrom of my work or ministry. I am sometimes bewildered and perplexed by rapid changes within society and around the world. So it is just as easy for me to get lost on the Christian journey as it is for anyone else.

Like you, I have sometimes wondered, "Is this all there is to life?" My forty-four years as a priest and thirty as a bishop have been marked by a search for the Lord, by a sincere concern to live life in accordance with his gospel. But, so often, my search seemed to lead me into darkness rather than light. I felt buffeted and bombarded by problems associated with my ministry. I often felt I was walking alone.

One day, while I was still archbishop of Cincinnati, I realized that I was constantly exhorting others to pray—frequently, daily. I was preaching often about the importance of prayer, about the significance of having a close relationship God. But I was not investing adequate time for prayer in my own life! A short time later, I had dinner with some priest friends of mine, who were themselves prayerful people. I shared my dilemma with them, and they advised me to act on my desire for adequate, quality time for prayer, affirming that this was, indeed, essential for the Christian life.

Fortunately, I followed their advice. With their encouragement and support, I resolved to devote an hour each day to prayer—the first hour each morning before the pressures of my ministry could get at me. Besides reciting the rosary and praying the Liturgy of the Hours, I have recourse to Scripture as a point of departure for meditative prayer.

During the early days of this new habit of prayer, I began to realize how often I had looked elsewhere for God rather than right in the midst of each day's journey! I became aware that often I sought escape from the difficulties and the suffering that I encountered daily in my ministry. I tended to think that my ministry was mine alone, rather than the Lord's.

In short, I came to recognize that I do *not* walk alone! God is with me. Through his word he helps to keep me on the right path. Through the breaking of bread each day, the risen Lord feeds the deepest hungers of my heart and spirit. And the Holy Spirit gives me what I need to carry out my pastoral ministry effectively.

I can assure you that my search for God continues, but I no longer search so far and wide. My quest takes me into the deepest recesses of my heart where I have learned to be still and listen to the Lord speaking to me in the events and people around me. I have come to understand the Lord's presence where, often before, I had experienced his absence. I have come to know myself—and accept myself—much more because of prayer.

I have also learned to recognize him in the "strangers" I encounter on my journey, that is, in my fellow pilgrims, in all my brothers and sisters. I know that they share my search, my dilemmas, and my deepest desires. From some of them I learn more about the Lord Jesus and his gospel. To others I proclaim the good news that I have heard and continue to hear.

In the past several years I have constantly tried to enter into closer communion with God through prayer, so that no part of my life, no part of myself, would be excluded from my relationship with the Lord. This search for union has been an exciting, life-giving, sustaining experience.

In the last two and a half years in particular, daily prayer has sustained me through two very different experiences, both of which are widely known.

The first was an accusation that, several years earlier, I had sexually abused a college seminarian by the name of Steven Cook. While I knew that the accusation was false, within hours it became a *cause célèbre* in the United States and around the world. Despite my innocence, I was totally humiliated and embarrassed. More important, the false accusation put my ministry in jeopardy, at least until the allegation was dropped. Before he died, Steven and I experienced a powerful, prayerful reconciliation.

The second event occurred when I learned in June 1995 that I had a malignant pancreatic tumor. Within days I underwent radical surgery followed by intensive radiation and chemotherapy. The unexpected news that I had an aggressive form of cancer meant that I had to face directly the prospect of an early death. While I remain cancer-free at this time, my perspective on my life and ministry has deepened because I have faced death in a way that I never did before.

Basically, it was my faith that made it possible for me to cope positively with these two events. As I faced these traumas, I literally felt God's presence. It was as if God was saying to me: "I will not abandon you. I will walk with you and help you through all of this." This has made an enormous difference in my life.

I have continued to find God in the events and persons of my daily life, and especially in moments of fear, anxiety, pain, and suffering. The crucified and risen Lord Jesus has become an intimate part of my daily life, the source of my strength, courage, and hope.

FREDERICK BUECHNER

is the author of twenty-seven works of fiction and nonfiction, including the autobiographical books Telling Secrets, Now and Then, The Sacred Journey, *as well as* The Alphabet of Grace, *which describes how grace often works through everyday events. His novel* Godric, *the story of a medieval monk, was nominated for the Pulitzer Prize. Mr. Buechner studied at the Union Theological Seminary in New York City and also served as a teacher and chaplain at Phillips Exeter Academy in New Hampshire during the 1960s. Today Mr. Buechner lives in Hobe Sound, Florida.*

Vocatus atque non vocatus, Deus aderit are the words C.G. Jung had chiseled into his stone lintel in Switzerland, which mean, freely translated, that you will eventually find God whether you want to or not. If you *want* to (even if you don't happen to believe He exists) all you have to do is find some quiet place, be quiet inside yourself, and ask Him to let you find Him (or Him you). As far as I know, it is a prayer that is always answered.

MYLES V. WHALEN, JR.,

a successful corporate attorney, was born in New York City and educated first by the Sisters of Charity, later by the Jesuits and finally at Harvard Law School, from which he was graduated in 1955. He practiced corporate law in New York City for many years, and served on numerous corporate boards before retiring in 1986.

Since his retirement Mr. Whalen has been very involved with a number of charitable organizations (working, as one example, for three years with the National Catholic AIDS Network). Mr. Whalen also teaches a course at the La Salle Academy in New York City, a middle school for talented but underprivileged children, many of whom are on public assistance. The course, which he teaches to the seventh and eighth graders, is called Introduction to Law. Besides all of these activities, he studies Spanish and watercolor painting.

When I speak of finding God I have in mind a very simple and quiet experience, but one that touches deeply and unforgettably. I believe that God is, in some way, "in" all things; at least all natural objects and phenomena and honest artistic efforts. In the simple yellow tulip, the setting sun, the potter's earnest bowl, the Sistine ceiling. If we can be quiet enough, each of these may put us in touch with the transcendent. But, for me, the clearest experiences of God have come in human encounters.

The encounter may go on for years—even a lifetime; or, two lives may intersect only once, fleetingly and in a way than an onlooker would consider insignificant or even odd. It is these latter—these "cameo appearances" that I would ask you to consider.

Haven't we all experienced a mutuality of respect, acceptance, affirmation, trust, and hope in a brief and simple meeting with a "perfect stranger"? And haven't we known that there was something holy about the experience?

I think of the young refugee taxi driver who, when asked, told me of the stifling life in Ceaucescu's Rumania and how he and his wife and brother-in-law had escaped sealed for three days in a wooden crate, leaving their infant son behind with grandparents, and of their years-long and eventually successful efforts to bring the child here. I remember the Afghan driver who refused to let me pay my fare because I had been interested in his story, and in the listening had, as he told me, become his friend. I think of the young Mexican counting and recounting his money at the subway entrance. He explained that he was five cents short of the fare and, and when I gave him a dollar because I had no change, he said that was too much. Then he said, "God bless you."

These are simple moments, but beautiful, and to find them we need only to be open to them: to the event and its echo. I think what we realize when we think back on such encounters is that not just one of us, but both of us, gave something and received something: something caring and respectful, trusting and hopeful. This, I believe, is one kind of encounter with God.

BROTHER BENET TVEDTEN, O.S.B.,

was born Denis Tvedten in Casselton, North Dakota. He graduated from St. John's University in Collegeville, Minnesota, in 1958 with a bachelor's degree in English. Two months later, at the age of twenty-one, he joined the Benedictine monastery of Blue Cloud Abbey at Marvin, South Dakota, and took the religious name Benet. Today he is the director of oblates of St. Benedict (laypeople affiliated with the monastery) and is involved in the monastery's retreat program. Brother Benet also served for ten years as the monastery's prior.

He has published fiction in various literary journals and is the author of All Manner of Monks. *"I enjoy the monastic life," Brother Benet remarked. "I've met an awful lot of delightful eccentrics and have made a lot of good friends."*

Now and then someone who professes no belief in God joins our group. As the months pass, this person eventually comes to believe in a Higher Power which is usually identified as God. Recovering alcoholics, too, know that their sobriety is a gift from God, a miracle. For God accomplishes in our lives whatever is humanly impossible. And so I think a conversation with a recovering alcoholic would benefit anyone who's having doubts about God's existence.

"I keep going to the abbey because that's where God lives."

These are the words of a recovering alcoholic who retreats here in the monastery where I've been a member for close to forty years. "Lives have been saved at the monastery," another recovering alcoholic tells me, "because of what's happened there on weekend retreats."

For these two men the monastery is a haven, a place where God is at work in the program of recovery. For me, the monastery was the place where I became a full-blown alcoholic. There is an old French drinking song that goes like this: "To drink like a Capuchin is to drink poorly, to drink like a Benedictine is to drink deeply, to drink like a Dominican is to drink pot after pot, but to drink like a Franciscan is to drink the cellar dry." I was imbued with my own Benedictine charism, as well as those of the other orders. I had it all. I also had the key to my community's liquor closet. In fact, I was in charge of the abbey's liquor supply.

"I think I have a problem with booze," I confessed to a nephew who was a chemical dependency counselor, "but I'll get a handle on it. I'm going to be living in Rome for three months. My daily habits will have to change over there." On a rainy Sunday afternoon in Rome, I slid down thirty-three steps on the Aventine and then recklessly staggered across streets with none of the fear I had of Roman drivers when I was stone sober. There is no geographical cure for alcoholism.

I found my way back to reality through Alcoholics Anonymous, which asked me to turn my will and life over to the care of God. I thought I'd done exactly that on the day of my solemn profession as a monk. By the time of my last drunk, I'd lost all sense of self-worth. I'd achieved a great degree of guilt and I wanted to die. Spiritually, I *was* dead.

In the Prologue to his *Rule*, Saint Benedict says, "The Lord waits for us daily to translate into action, as we should, his holy teachings. Therefore our life span has been lengthened by way of a truce, that we may amend our misdeeds." *The Rule of St. Benedict* and the AA program teach me to live one day at a time. I've been amazed by the parallels. At an AA meeting early in my recovery, I mentioned a problem I was having. A woman asked me, "Do you pray?" I was surprised and indignant that she should ask such a question. "Of course I pray. I'm a professional prayer. I'm a monk." What she meant, in the language of AA, was: "Have you been entirely ready to have God remove your defects? Have you improved your conscious contact with God through humble prayer? Have you prayed only for knowledge of His will and the power to carry it out?" In the background, I heard Benedict asking, "Have you prayed not in a loud voice, but with tears and heartfelt devotion?"

"We are willing to grow along spiritual lines," AA states. "The principles we have set down are guides to progress. We claim spiritual progress rather than spiritual perfection." Recovery is a process. So is being a monk. St. Benedict does not demand spiritual perfection. Monks follow his *Rule* in order to achieve "some degree of virtue." Sanctity is not required in either Alcoholics Anonymous or the Order of St. Benedict. The day-by-day effort to become a better person is the only requirement. St. Benedict calls this gradual conversion. AA calls it "working the program."

On the day I decided to sober up, I turned over my liquor closet key to the abbot. I've not had to go back into that closet for fifteen years. Another monk recovering from alcoholism has written: "The alcoholic monk, by the time he has reached the final stage of the disease, is spiritually, psychologically, and physically devastated." This, of course, is true of every alcoholic. We are restored to health by recovering our spirituality. For me this meant becoming a Benedictine all over again. We all go back to what was once so familiar in our lives. "We are willing to grow along spiritual lines." What was lost is found when we admit our powerlessness. "There is one who has all power. That one is God. May you find him now."

Saint Benedict reminded me: "What, dear brothers, is more delightful than this voice of the Lord calling us? See how the Lord in his love shows us the way of life."

Christopher Isherwood found that some people are like countries. "When you are with them, that is your country and you speak its language. And then it does not matter where you are together, you are at home." I've found other countries where I'm welcomed. There are other groups of people whose language I speak. And I'm happy being back at home in the monastery. It is indeed the place where God lives.

HELEN M. ALVARÉ

is a mother, an attorney, and a theologian. She serves as director of planning and information for the National Conference of Catholic Bishops' Secretariat for Pro-Life Activities in Washington, D.C., acting as spokesperson for pro-life issues in the Catholic Church. In that capacity, she has appeared frequently on television, as well as in national magazines and newspapers.

Before this position, Ms. Alvaré had worked for three years as a corporate litigator for a Philadelphia law firm. But while she enjoyed her work as an attorney, she found herself wanting to do more for people and her church. "I thought that if my religion is the most important thing in my life, and if I'm going to be spending ten or twelve hours a day working, why shouldn't the two be more like one?" After leaving her job in Philadelphia, she came to Washington on a full scholarship at the Catholic University of America, to begin a master's degree in theology. In 1990, during her second year of doctoral studies, she began her work with the Bishops' Conference. Today Ms. Alvaré lives in Maryland with her husband and young daughter.

God is often at work in finding *you* in experiences of being loved by people whose actions far transcend our limited expectations of what is owed to us in the name of merely human justice or fairness. Your small child jumps into your arms and kisses you just for being her mother; your husband leaves you a sweet note when you arrive home late at night after work. One glimpses God's amazing kindness in these expressions of love that confound the merely worldly notions of what human beings owe to one another.

God is also present in the experience of witnessing the transforming power of the word of God. Even when the word is spoken by ordinary women and men, in ordinary ways and settings, one watches in awe to see lives touched, changed, and moved. It is unexpected, inexplicable, in the tiny framework of human reason; but in a framework that includes God, it is gift and encounter.

HOWARD ESBIN,

after twenty-five years of working in various businesses—retailing, marketing, and executive training—decided that he wanted to work in more of what he called a "service-oriented field." So, in 1990, after receiving his master's degree in education from McGill University, he began his work with the Canadian International Development Agency, a job that eventually landed him a three-year stint in East Africa working in small business development. Today Howard lives in Montreal, and is managing director of Bridgehead-Oxfam America Trading, an organization that assists self-help groups from marginalized communities in the developing world. He is also busy finishing his doctoral work in education at McGill.

Howard was raised by Jewish parents in Brooklyn, but as part of his career change he traveled to Tibet and North India for spiritual retreats, as well as to various parts of North America exploring Native American spirituality. "I was trying to redefine my career goals, and at the same time there was also some stuff going on inside me," he explains. "Now, I pray everywhere."

What woman or man, at one time or another, hasn't imagined discovering a secret trove of gold and becoming forever free of material want? This dream is rooted within each of us. And it stems from the belief that this "precious, yellow, non-rusting, malleable, ductile, metallic element of high density, used as a fundamental monetary medium" (as the Oxford Dictionary would have it) makes the world go round. The more one possesses the more secure one becomes and the more one is able to satisfy any desire at all.

Yet this basic impulse is thwarted and debased all the time. Witness the universal consequences of greed and exploitation. Consider the staggering fortunes squandered daily in chance games against implausible odds. An image of the golden calf in Exodus comes to mind; the one set up and worshiped by many of my ancient forbears.

There is, then, a mysterious and profound interrelationship between gold and God. This is consciously alluded to on United States currency where every coin and bill is inscribed "In God We Trust." How we come to perceive this relationship dictates where we focus attention and effort in our lives. As the saying goes, "a hungry person sees only bread."

Sufis state that God created the universe out of love. The Holy Quran bears this out by describing God as a "hidden treasure longing to be known." The believer accepts the omnipresence and indivisibility of God throughout life. Devout Jews affirm that "God is One," and devout Muslims affirm "There is no God but God."

From this purview God is the living source of all existence in its every manifestation, from the subatomic to the extra cosmic. We humans, along with all other living things from the single-cell organism to forms beyond our ken, are creatures marvelously made by God. The very fibre of our being, therefore, is the stuff of God.

Considering the seemingly infinite multiplicity of things, tangible and subtle, which fills our consciousness, God's essential unity and purposefulness easily and often becomes lost from sight. Nevertheless, the believer remembers that every single thing, idea, and experience remains rooted to the Creator and, through its singularity, expresses the Divine imprint. Therefore, anything pursued long enough and intently enough will ultimately lead back to the source.

In this context we can intuit why gold's special properties so uniquely reflect God's preciousness and how easily blinded we can become in pursuing the former while hungering for the latter. The interplay between Spirit and Matter is such that anything conceivable becomes possible—including the alchemist's quest to transmute lead into gold. This, however, will mean one thing to the materialist and quite another to the seeker after God.

In the Judeo-Christian tradition the angels must praise and worship God while we humans have a choice to do so or not. Consequently, despite God's longing for remembrance and recognition, we can remain purposefully or ignorantly immersed in the world of appearances. At any point, however, we can come to acknowledge what Hazrat Inayat Khan calls "the cause behind the cause" and thereby experience, in the words of William Blake, "heaven in a grain of sand and eternity in a flower."

So to anyone who asks of me how they might find God, my answer must be this: There are as many paths to God as there are people living in the world. Each must discover and follow his own. It matters not how you seek God as long as you seek. It matters not how you think of God as long as you think. And it matters not how you love God, as long as you love. For, sooner or later, God will find you.

REV. JOHN EUDES BAMBERGER, O.C.S.O.,

has been since 1957 abbot of the Trappist Abbey of the Genesee in Piffard, New York. Dom John Eudes, a psychiatrist, joined the Cistercian Order in 1950 at the Abbey of Our Lady of Gethsemani in Kentucky, where he studied with Thomas Merton.

I happen to live in a setting where God seems to be everywhere; He is in nature in an unending variety of ways, from the marvelous forms of trees to the beauty of complex organic chemical structures. But above all, God lives within the human spirit.

That is why I believe that the most fruitful place to search for God is at the center of the soul of the person you love most personally and so most purely; with the greatest respect for the uniqueness and well-being of that person. We cannot find that center of the other without discovering, reflexively in our own spirit, the same presence, the same uniqueness that strives to honor the goodness that is the other. There is an elusive presence that forms the ground of any truly personal exchange with another. When the other is the most loved, that presence becomes less elusive: It takes on a density that is more readily recognized as being transcendent to the beloved and to my love. It casts a brighter light, can be felt as the atmosphere that envelops the person of the beloved. To perceive something of this radiance that is at the heart of human life, affirming, knowing, and creating what is most precious of all things, the One Beloved, is to know that there is an infinite, transcendent, living God who is the secret answer to the mystery of the human heart. Look intently, in quiet, with desire to see what is most desirable in what you desire, and you will find it quite natural to believe that God *is*.

DEOTHA ARMSTRONG,

at the age of six, was sent by her Methodist parents to a Catholic school in their Harlem neighborhood. The following year Dee decided she wanted to make her First Communion along with her classmates. One of the nuns told her that this might prove difficult since her parents might not approve. So Dee decided to ask her parents to become Catholics. "But you're only eight years old!" said the nun. "But what's the problem?" said Dee, "God is God all over." Dee's parents decided to attend instructional classes at the church and eventually decided to become Catholics. "But my Methodist grandmother was furious," remembers Dee. "She just never appreciated confession in a little box."

After Dee had worked thirty-one years for the same company in New York City, she was laid off. In 1984 she began working for St. Aloysius Church in Harlem. She is currently separated from her husband of forty-one years. "But we're still the best of friends," she says. Dee has raised one child, Laverne, now age thirty-nine, and is the proud grandmother of Joi and Britany. Rather than writing out her response, Dee preferred to answer the question orally, in what turned out to be a lively monologue.

First of all, everybody has *some* kind of problem in their life. And you usually find God when things aren't all good. Usually, when there's a problem in your life you're looking for some sort of help, some kind of connection, because it's a heavy burden. And I always feel you should be able to go directly to God. Because, first of all, he made you, so he knows you better than *anybody*. He loves you. And all he is doing is waiting for you to ask him.

Now, he's not a fast person, he is a sure person. Swiftness is *not* his best thing. So you have to realize that when you ask him to help you, it will not be done in the next breath. Sometimes it is, but nine times out of ten it will be done in *his* time, not your time. But you have to have that faith to know that he will come to your rescue. Regardless of what it is. It could be something as simple as looking for a shoestring. You're in your house looking for that shoestring and saying, "God, where is that *shoestring*?" And you look up and down and say, "Look, Lord, you know where it is. Help me out. I need this!" And sure enough, you find it. Now you can say, "Oh, it was here all the time," but hey, did he come through?

When it comes to looking for God, if you even don't know what to look for, I would say that you're looking for peace of mind. Here's a situation: After working for an insurance company for thirty-one years I was fired. I was devastated. You know…thirty-one years of your life, and then someone calls you in one afternoon and says, "You no longer work here!" *What?*

At that point you're really in a dilemma. You know that this is your livelihood. What are you going to do? Who can you turn to?

When the man was firing me, I said to him, "I can't believe this is true, but I don't believe God would allow you to close this door—which is my bread and butter—unless he had another door to open. So, knowing that he must have another door, and it *has* to be better than this after thirty-one years, I will leave and walk out of here knowing that he must have something else better for me." And, of course, he thought, "Oh yeah, that's a beautiful outlook," but I was serious.

True, I'm blessed because I know I can turn to God. But let's say you don't even know if he *exists* or not, OK? Now, if someone approaches me—and people have after something drastic happens—and says, "What am I going to do?" I'd say, first of all, you *have* to just sit yourself down and get yourself together. And the only person who knows you better than anybody is God, whether you believe it or not. Remember, you would not be in this world if he didn't make you. So you would go to the Creator. It's just like if you wanted a dress, you'd go to the dressmaker, if you wanted your hair done, you'd go to the hairdresser. So let's go to the beginning of this situation: Let's go to God.

Now, what do you say when you get there? You just speak on the situation. Not that he doesn't *know* the situation! He is *well* aware of the situation. But you need to voice it and let it come out of you. You need to say, "God, I am in trouble, I need some help. Please help me." Now, I was once told by a priest—and it's good advice—that when you're in big trouble sometimes you don't know how to pray, but "Lord, have mercy" is more than sufficient.

You know, you wouldn't be here without God. If God didn't breathe life into your mother's womb, well, believe me, you wouldn't be here. So let's go back to him. Just say, "Lord, I'm in trouble. I don't know you, I don't know about you, but can you help me? And, above all, if you just help me through, I will try to learn about you." Believe me, he *hears* that. Now, like I said, sometimes it doesn't work overnight, but more than likely he will get to you, and you will see a change of some sort, and that will encourage you on this road that you have started down.

William E. Simon

was Secretary of the Treasury from 1974 to 1977 under Presidents Richard Nixon and Gerald Ford. Prior to this position, Mr. Simon had a long and distinguished business career, and served as senior partner at Salomon Brothers. He is currently chairman of William E. Simon & Sons, New Jersey, and president of the John M. Olin Foundation.

How can I find God? This is the everlasting question that every thinking person must confront at some time in his or her life. That we become ill, grow old, and die means that we will never rest entirely content with our material and secular achievements. Our human condition leads us back to basic spiritual questions: What is God and how do we find Him?

Thankfully, the answers to those questions do not depend on us alone. I believe that God, in His infinite wisdom, mercy, and patience, allows all of us, believers and nonbelievers alike, opportunities to find Him along our own paths in life.

So there is not one answer, but many, and each brings its own value and honors God in a unique way. My own perspective is drawn more from practical experience, rather than philosophical speculation. I am a lifelong Catholic who began to know God as an altar boy, and have drawn closer to Him, as my family and I became more active in our faith.

And what I have come to see, and probably more belatedly

and imperfectly than He would like, is that God is alive in every person. His spirit may burn more brightly, or more steadily, in some people, but it is present in all of us. I believe this because I have seen it throughout my life, but most recently and most powerfully as a eucharistic minister at Morristown Memorial Hospital, Memorial Sloan-Kettering Cancer Center, and the Cardinal Cooke Health Care Center in New York City. I find God within the walls of these hospitals as I attend to the welfare and needs of people, many of whom are terminally ill, and always alone and searching.

As an active Knight of Malta, I became involved as a eucharistic minister in order to comfort and console many who are on the doorstep of death. They want to talk. They want to visit. Some are sad and take comfort in shared words of prayer. Many cry, overjoyed, as I pour holy water from Lourdes on their bodies. It is during these times that I feel a closeness to God.

During these visits, I have become humbled by the faith that the patients demonstrate as they look to God for strength. These people, young and old, are afflicted with fatal illnesses, yet they are at peace with God and with themselves. They have come to know their Creator and deepened their faith that He will be with them, not only in this life but also in the world beyond. Many times I have come away from the hospital wondering if I have given the sick and infirm half of what they've given me. I have seen in their eyes that God isn't everything—He's the only thing. When I see God's divine work in these people, I feel profoundly grateful to them for helping me to strengthen my own faith.

On one occasion, I was visiting a young man who was dying of AIDS. His body was pitifully thin, racked with pain. As we prayed together, I looked down on this poor soul and remembered Christ's words—whatsoever you do for the least of my brethren, you have done for me.

I've thought about that moment several times since. And I realize that I was not just looking into the face of that young man—I was looking directly into the eyes of Christ.

So, one answer to the question "Where and how do we find God?" might be: almost everywhere—in fact, many times right in front of us, if we just open our eyes and hearts to let Him in.

SARAH ELLSWORTH,

thirty-eight, is a nurse-midwife living on the Navaho reservation in northwest New Mexico. After graduating from Smith College in 1981, Sarah did hospice work, visiting sick and dying patients in their homes. She received her master's degree in the science of nursing from Yale University in 1986 and began work as a midwife in the inner city of New Haven, Connecticut.

Sarah lives with her companion, Art Heller, a veterinarian, and their two-year-old son, Perin, who, as Sarah says, "is the purest expression of God I have ever encountered."

Despite having been raised by an atheist and an agnostic, I've always believed that God exists and is manifested everywhere. So, how to find this omnipresent Being? First awaken your mind from the drowsy numbness of everyday adult life through daily meditation. Focus on a mantra, a light, or your breath. Let your thoughts gently fall away. Slowly you'll begin to palpate, in that inner silence, a certain connectedness. Your sense of isolation, of alienation, will fade. The frenetic monkey of your mind will still and become clear. Then, open your eyes. Reach with your heart. There: in that rock, in that ant, in that child's openness and wonder, in that abusive husband, in his abused wife, in the unfurling leaves of spring, in your annoying co-worker, in your thoughts, in birth, in death—there is God.

Try to hold this awareness throughout the day. Moving through the world becomes your worship. Caring for the earth and its inhabitants becomes your prayer. And understanding and forgiving our enemies becomes an opportunity for spiritual growth.

BETTY AND BILL BAUMANN,

it can be fairly stated, have led a most interesting life together. They met in college, fixed up on a blind date—since both were applying to the Peace Corps. Married in the summer of 1966, they began their service in Colombia, South America, working in rural cooperative development, helping an artisan town of basket weavers. After returning to the United States in 1970, both were hired to work as counselors in community mental health centers in Philadelphia. This lasted for a few years, with Bill resigning in 1972, to work full time salvaging a run-down house that they shared with a dozen or so people. "We shared communal meals, that sort of thing," says Bill.

Next, the two worked in Mexico, heading up a team of eight international volunteers with the American Friends Service Committee, working among the Otomi Indians. After returning once again to Philadelphia, Betty completed her master's degree in social work and Bill his master's in anthropology. Their son, Emil, was born in 1976. During the 1980s Bill and Betty worked in refugee camps in Central America (independently, while the other stayed home with Emil). Beginning in 1992 the family of three moved to Kenya with the Mennonite Central Committee to work in Sudan, Ethiopia, Somalia, Kenya, Tanzania, and Uganda, promoting self-help craft projects. They returned again to the States in June 1995 and continue their volunteer work with the Mennonites.

> *"Some day," says Betty, "we'll get 'real' again and earn a livelihood."

BETTY:

I guess my first response to the question is that there is no *one* God, but that God is an essence within each human being. Sometimes this presence is recognized and sometimes not—but how unfortunate are they who are unaware of this.

Many people have a problem with seeing or knowing God because it somehow conjures up a religious sect or specific set of beliefs that they find restricting. But, for me, God is a magnificent power or presence that we can turn to for comfort or rejoice with in gladness. In my own case, as a practicing Catholic, God takes on both a wider and more precise presence: the Father, the Son, and the Holy Spirit in one being—a miraculous Trinity who my shared community treats in a ritualistic manner that brings deep meaning to my personal life. But that's me, and I know God's presence is there for all humankind and is reflected in each and every one of us as creatures of the Supreme Being.

How can we find God? For many North Americans it seems that the question is merely rhetorical. How do we answer for the extremely advantageous and privileged life we lead as compared to the vast majority of peoples on this earth? What have we done, or more importantly what are we expected to do, in order to deserve a life so full of comforts (water, food, shelter, telephones, entertainment, clothing, gadgets, education, participatory political systems, alternatives and options abounding)? If we are somehow a favored people for the moment, aren't we called into the world community to give back some of the wealth and surplus of our good fortune? I just know that for myself when I reach out to another, there is nothing in the world that brings me such contentment and satisfaction. This is when God is closest to me or me to God—when I am in a relationship with others, the children of God.

So God, or the Supreme Being or Presence, is within each and every one of us. Look at us, look at the intricacy of how we are assembled; look at the complexity of our individual selves. Surely there is a wondrous being and presence who maintains all human beings!

But to return to the original question: How can I find God? God is everywhere and within everything. God is you, how you perceive the world around you; how you relate to other living things around you; how you share your benefits with those around you; how you seek comfort from those around you. God is not abstract, but neither is God housed in some building. It is just a matter of accepting that you and I have a really good buddy, in union with us (like a Siamese twin who experiences and feels all that we do) who is *always* there, in good and bad, sad and glad. And that buddy will never, ever turn against us or reject us. With that knowledge, how loved and accepted and powerful we can become to ourselves.

So, to one seeking God, I would reassure you that God is *not* organized religion. And God is *not* scriptures and holy books and rules and regulations. God is the spirit within us and within all our fellow human beings, waiting patiently to be recognized, and there for us to draw upon as needed. For me, God is the greatest gift we have, and the beauty is that God is there for absolutely everyone.

BILL:

Do you pray? Do you meditate? Do you quietly talk to yourself when trying to work through a problem? If so, you have already found God. God is there, right there. He is present in all good acts and in all good things. He is the force behind life. You can find or recognize God as long as you don't have too narrow a notion of what He/She looks like. God is with every person who embraces peace, kindness, and generosity. Any time you reach out to me or I to you, we have found God. He is present.

I firmly believe that He has given *us* the latitude to describe Him as we wish, or permission to talk to Him as we are able, because of the nature of the diversity of the human family. We are, however, accountable and may not abuse this possession of God within ourselves to the exclusion or judgment of others' path to finding God. If my notion of God is different from your notion of God—that's OK. But if, because we differ on who or what God is, we don't speak or reach out to one another—that's a problem.

When I lived in the Muslim world, in Sudan, I was extended great courtesy and respect, and I was touched by God—through the Muslims—in all these occasions. Refreshing tea in the heat of the day, a comfortable, shaded place to rest when I was fatigued, an assistance in communicating with a merchant in the market, the invitation to share a meal at sunset during the Ramadan fast, and on and on. God seemed to be more obviously present in simple and humble people, and to distance myself from them for whatever reason was to minimize the chances or opportunities to see God. My Christian beliefs or my "Christianity," far from being an obstacle to communication with Muslims, was a vehicle and an asset to understanding our shared humanity.

Friends have often asked me how I was able to "get through" to so-and-so, or find anything of interest in this or that person. My response is: They are God. If they are repulsive, threatening, distant, or downright difficult—then they are surely God's test. God is challenging me to find Him in this or that person, and when I do, everything changes. For all the loftiness in which we shroud God and His presence, He is to be found in our humanness—our *shared* humanity—and that's the miracle. That's the part which eludes us and that we have such trouble comprehending. No *one* individual or group or congregation can claim

God as theirs. He exists in all people of faith and trust. He can be found and spoken to simply by opening our hearts to all of humankind without conditions. And in the act of doing this, we find God.

MARY HIGGINS CLARK

has been called "America's Queen of Suspense." She is the top-selling woman suspense writer in the United States and the author of sixteen bestsellers, including Where Are the Children?, A Stranger Is Watching, The Cradle Will Fall, Remember Me, Moonlight Becomes You, *and* My Gal Sunday: Henry and Sunday Stories. *She has received numerous prizes—literary and otherwise—including France's* Grand Prix de Littérature.

Ms. Clark was left a young widow by the death of her husband, Warren, from a heart attack in 1964. Having already published a few short stories, she began writing radio scripts and eventually decided to write books. Every morning, Ms. Clark rose at 5 A.M., and wrote until 7 A.M., when she readied her children for school. Catching up on her formal education, Ms. Clark graduated from Fordham University in 1979 with a bachelor's degree in philosophy. In 1996 she married John J. Conheeney, a retired investments executive. Ms. Clark has five children and six grandchildren. Today she lives with her husband in Saddle River, New Jersey.

If someone were to ask me how to find God, I think I would answer with another question: Why are you asking? Is it because there is a restlessness in your very being that urges you to seek, to find the source of your existence?

A philosopher once wrote about "the footsteps of God." I believe that those footsteps are imbedded in our souls, and we will not be at peace until we learn to follow them.

Then I would suggest that you don't need one special place to look, because the handwork of God surrounds you. Consider the harmony of nature. Are the branches of the trees lush with green leaves and filled with nests, or are they becoming orange and copper and auburn? Are they bare, their occupants instinctively winged to more hospitable climates? Or are those same trees suddenly surrounded with the faint pink haze that signals the arrival of spring? To witness the change of seasons is, I believe, to find God, and to echo the words of the hymn, "How great Thou art."

Let's now peek into a crib where a newborn infant is sleeping, exhausted from its journey of nine months. Pick up the baby. Feel its breath on your neck. Yearn over its helplessness and realize that with the swiftly passing years it may well become the staff of the parents who are nurturing it now. I think that you can find God in the miracle of the cycle of life.

And day follows night. The sun rises and sets. Tides lap at the shore and recede, all in perfect harmony with each other.

There may indeed have been a "big bang." But who caused it? Thomas Aquinas said that belief in God is not in opposition to science. Then he speaks of the "uncaused cause," the God you are seeking.

Finally, think about your own life. Realize that all the good, all the love you have known, has been the gift of the Eternal Good. And then begin your journey of faith with these words: "I believe. Lord, help my unbelief."

Rev. Daniel J. Harrington, S.J.,

is professor of Sacred Scripture at the Weston Jesuit School of Theology in Cambridge, Massachusetts. Father Harrington, an internationally recognized Scripture scholar, is general editor of the journal New Testament Abstracts *and the* Sacra Pagina *series of books, and the author of numerous scholarly articles and books, including* Interpreting the New Testament: A Practical Guide *and* How to Read the Gospels. *He is former president of the Catholic Biblical Association of America and has been a member of the Society of Jesus since 1958.*

I find God largely in and through the Bible. Most of my academic, spiritual, and pastoral life revolves around the Bible. It is for me the most important way to come to know, love, and serve God.

My love for the Bible goes back a long way. I stutter. I always have, and I guess I always will. As a young boy I read in a newspaper that Moses stuttered. I looked it up in the Bible, and sure enough in Exodus 4:10 Moses says to God: "I am slow of speech and slow of tongue." But I found much more in Exodus 3–4. It is the story of God's self-revelation to Moses at Mount Horeb. It tells about the burning bush, the suffering of God's people Israel in Egypt, the revelation of the special divine name ("I am who I am"), God's promise of liberation from slavery, Moses' miraculous powers, and God's call to Moses to speak on God's behalf. I read that story over and over, and it gradually worked upon me so that it has shaped my religious consciousness to this day. As a boy of ten or eleven years of age I found God in the Bible, and I have continued to do so ever since.

As a Jesuit priest and professor of biblical studies, I have been able to blend my profession and my love for the Bible. Many of my happiest personal experiences have taken place in the academic study of the Bible: reading the first chapter of John's Gospel in Greek, beginning the study of Hebrew, earning a doctorate in biblical languages and cultures from Harvard University, teaching Scripture to theology students, and preaching on the Scriptures every Sunday for over twenty-five years. As general editor of *New Testament Abstracts* since 1972, I see everything in the academic study of the New Testament. The Bible never grows wearisome or stale for me. I am deeply in love with the Bible as God's word.

Those who find God in the Bible often surround their experience with theological terms, such as inspiration, revelation, inerrancy, canon, authority, and normativity. These terms have long histories and name significant theological realities. But more fundamental is the hermeneutical process that I illustrated above with reference to Exodus 3–4.

We bring to the biblical text ourselves, our experiences, our personal strengths and limits, our communal and individual identities. The Bible itself is a collection of books, written at different times and in different places. The Old Testament contains narratives about ancient Israel's patriarchs and kings, law codes, prophetic oracles, songs of praise and laments, proverbs, wisdom instructions, love poems, and apocalyptic visions. The New Testament consists of four accounts of Jesus' life and teachings, stories about the apostles, letters from Paul and other early Christian writers, and an apocalyptic prophecy.

Biblical scholars try to understand the books of Scripture with the methods of literary, historical, and theological analysis. They make available tools that enable readers today to understand and appreciate the text better than they could do on their own. And yet the Bible is not simply an object of antiquarian research or words on a page (no matter how sacred). In the encounter between the reader and the text, the "word of God" comes alive. Something can and does happen. In that encounter—whether it takes the form of silent or oral reading, literary analysis, or preaching, the word of God comes alive for me. I see analogies, points of contact, between what the biblical text describes and my life. As I discover and articulate those analogies, I develop a language for thinking and talking about the experience of God and about human existence. This in turn shapes my way of living and how I interact with others. And the whole circle of experience, biblical texts, assimilation of the text, and praxis—the hermeneutical circle—begins again.

The "word of God" is not identical with the text of the Bible. For me, it refers to the whole process of encountering God in and through the Scriptures. From the Bible we come to know the God of our religious tradition and what it means to be God's people. With the help of the psalms, we learn to express both our thanks and praise to God, as well as our sadness and anger. We find what hope means through the prophets and seers. We meet Jesus of Nazareth whom we confess to be the "Word of God." In and through the Word/word, God tells us who God is and what God wants us to be and do. The epistles show what it means to live out Christian faith amidst the realities of a sometimes dangerous and hostile world—one, nevertheless, under the sovereignty of God and his Messiah.

The encounter with God through the Bible cannot be programmed or forced. According to the Bible (and especially Exodus 3–4), God takes the initiative in this relationship and leads us where God wants us to go. There is, however, an ancient, simple, and effective framework for facilitating encounter with God through the Bible. It is often called by its Latin name *lectio divina* ("divine, or spiritual, reading").

There are four steps in *lectio divina*: reading (What does the text say?), meditation (What is God saying to me through this text?), prayer (What do I want to say to God on the basis of this text?), and action (What difference can this text make in how I act? What possibilities does it open up? What challenges does it pose?).

The God of the Bible is the God of Jesus Christ. I experience this God in and through the Bible and my life. It is my privilege as a Jesuit priest to study and teach Scripture, to proclaim and preach God's word, and to celebrate the Church's liturgies (which are largely cast in the language of the Bible). In the midst of these wonderful activities (which are my greatest joy), I occasionally stutter. And this brings me back to where my spiritual journey with the Bible began. Though I am slow of speech and tongue like Moses, I still hear the words of Exodus 4:11–12: "Who gives speech to mortals? Who makes them mute or deaf, seeing or blind? Is it not I, the LORD? Now go, and I will be with your mouth and teach you what you are to speak."

Rabbi Peter J. Rubinstein

is the senior rabbi of Central Synagogue in New York City, a Reform congregation affiliated with the Union of American Hebrew Congregations. Prior to his work in New York, Rabbi Rubinstein served as rabbi of synagogues in San Mateo, California, and White Plains, New York.

Rabbi Rubinstein received his bachelor's degree from Amherst College and was ordained from the Hebrew Union College-Hebrew Institute of Religion in New York City, where he received a master of Hebrew Letters degree. After ordination he spent three years as a Fellow at the Hebrew Union College-Jewish Institute of Religion in Cincinnati, Ohio, specializing in the history of the Jewish community during the Second Commonwealth. He has held teaching positions at HUC-JIR, Manhattanville College, and Colgate University. Rabbi Rubinstein lives in New York City with his wife, Kerry Bradford, a management consultant. They have two children, Michael, twenty-five, and Noah, twenty-two.

I suppose that rabbis are heralded to be God experts. It surely is an idea with which I grew up, one which almost prohibited my considering the rabbinate as my life's work. It was difficult, probably still is, to believe that I really know about God.

God hasn't "called" me or spoken to me, at least not that I'm aware. I remember when one of my sons caught me off guard and challenged me with the question "Dad, where is God?" My instinctively brilliant rabbinic response was "Go ask your mother!"

It's difficult to find God, and I suppose that you will look only if you have time on your hands. Some of us may remember when "finding yourself" was the personal mission of an entire generation. It was a worthwhile aspiration but it was ultimately an indulgent search. People who are hungry, seeking work, and caring for dying loved ones don't have the time or energy for finding themselves or anyone else. They simply do what it takes to survive, putting one foot in front of the other, taking one step at a time.

Because "finding" one's self smacks of a process with no defined finale, I am concerned that finding God depends upon a need to *find* God, not simply a need to *look* for God. I have an embroidered pillow in my office with a clearly stated theology. It says "Nothing improves our prayer life faster than big trouble." I think people who really need God, I mean *really* need God, manage to find God or else give up the search and withdraw from it.

You will find God when you believe that you have been found by God. Anyone who has played hide-and-seek will understand how this works. There is no game if the "hider" cannot be found. Sometimes the hider needs to reveal himself or herself in order to be found.

I would tell the Jew who is looking for God to read history, our history. There is where God intends to be found. The miracle of Jewish survival, improbable as it is, attests to God. Consider the Exodus, our being given the commandments, the idea of *B'rit* (Covenant) and the enduring values which are part of each historical circumstance.

I am stunned by Jewish history. It is where I have found God and where I would counsel others to begin. Then I would turn the seeker to his/her own life history to find a miracle there as well. Consider the countless coincidences that resulted in your personal creation. Sensitive reflection will move you to celebrate your own "being" and uniqueness and permit you to hear the voices and longings of your ancestors. They will also speak of God.

I find God everywhere, but I begin in history. From high school I remember laws of physics that indicate how you can predict how an object will move once you know the forces and vectors which act upon it. God is that way. We may only know where to look for God when we fully understand the forces that have led us to this moment. We need to know why we are looking, why we feel compelled to find God. We need to know our history, and we need to internalize emotionally the mystery and miracle of our own being. And when all is said and done, we may only find God when we are no longer looking. God may emerge in the best and worst moments of our lives, when there is nothing else left.

THE CHILDREN OF ST. THOMAS SCHOOL

When she read the original article in America *magazine, Jean Shea, who teaches computer skills at the St. Thomas School in Crystal Lake, Illinois, thought that the question "How Can I Find God?" might be a good one to use for a typing exercise in class. "I try to make the word processor interesting to all ages," she explained.*

After some consideration, Mrs. Shea decided that her seventh-grade class would be an ideal class to answer the question. A few of their answers follow.

I find God in babies because they express love, kindness, and gentleness. Babies symbolize God because babies are gentle and loving, and can always make you smile. They are very innocent, just like God.

When babies are young they may not be able to speak, but you always know what they are feeling. And although you cannot talk to them physically, you can still show them your love. For example, by treating them with care. If you talk to babies and they don't talk back, you still know they love you. I think that's how it is with God.

Allison Janik

I find God in everything, but mostly in animals. They help me in everything, like in hard times. I always thought I can talk to the animals. A river otter is one of my favorite animals. I think I resemble a river otter's personality. They love water just like I do. Indians hunted the river otter. Indians hunt for food, and I hunt for good grades and special feelings. When I look at people like Indians, I find God. God is trusting, loving, and caring. River otters, Indians, and all of us are all alike, because we are all hunting for God.

Robert Schrempf

I find God within myself and the people I meet and within their actions, such as sharing, caring, loving, and teaching. I find God in the sports I play, such as when I hit a home run.

I also found God when I hurt my arm. I never knew how much I used my arm that was broken until God showed me how much I use my left arm.

I can also find God when I am alone and all by myself, and when our class is saying prayers. God can be anywhere from the smallest place to the biggest place, such as the Sistine Chapel. So wherever you want him to be, He will be there.

Tom Seithel

I find God mostly in nature. Sometimes when I go fishing, I feel like God is with me because I feel so calm going away from my house. I also think God is with me because even if it is raining, there is always a little sunshine in the water. I also find God whenever I see an animal in the wild. I feel as if they are representatives of God. I like that.

Billy Stanton

I find God in kids and babies. I think it's neat to see how kids grow, not only on the outside, but how they grow smarter and grow on the inside too. Kids can always cheer you up. You can really see a miracle in children.

I have a cousin, Bernadette, who reminds me of this. I have seen her grow up from when she was born to now, age four. She is very special because she is alive. She had whooping cough when she was a baby and was in a coma. It was amazing that she lived. We are all very happy to have her, and now she has a baby sister who is very healthy.

Jackie Chybik

I find God almost anywhere, in school, in football, in basketball, and in baseball. In the sports I play God protects me from being injured or killed. He helps me succeed and to fulfill my sports dreams. He encourages me to try my hardest and do my best. I also find God in my friends. They help me if I am doing something wrong or feeling bad.

In school God helps me get good grades. Also, in the morning we say prayers and have special intentions to pray for people who need to be prayed for.

Thank you, God, for all the good things you do for me!

Mike Marx

I find God in my friends. They are always there for me when I'm down. My friends will always be there if I need a laugh or am bored. Friends help you when you need advice, just like God would. With friends you can open up and tell them a lot of things that you can't tell your mom and dad. With a true friend, you don't have to worry about your secrets getting out into the public.

I find God in the earth and its features. Nature will always be there if I need to cool down. When the earth blooms, it is truly magical to see all the colors of fall. This makes me feel loved and warm inside. The squirrels gathering fruits and nuts is truly a work of God. All creation working together looks like my image of heaven.

Jim Gray

I find God through dogs because dogs are full of love. They always make you feel better when you feel down. They make you feel special and loved. Dogs protect and guide you and give you companionship, just like God.

I have a dog at home named Mollie. When I go home at night I play with her, and she always brightens up my day.

Like I said, dogs are always there for you. If you take care of them, they will take care of you. Even though dogs cannot talk, they still love, just like God.

Katie Drury

Sister Mary Rose McGeady, D.C.,

is president of Covenant House, an organization that provides food, clothing, shelter, and medical care to forty-one thousand adolescents under the age of twenty-one each year. Sister Mary Rose, a member of the Daughters of Charity of St. Vincent de Paul, has worked for over thirty years in childcare and mental healthcare. From 1981 to 1987, she served as regional superior of the Daughters of Charity. Sister Mary Rose lives with her religious community in the Bedford-Stuyvesant section of Brooklyn, New York.

To assist those with little awareness of faith in their lives to "find God" is often an awesome task. For our adolescents whose life experience is characterized by abuse and negativism, it is especially challenging to present the picture of a giving, loving God in their lives. One way we often find effective is to have them reflect on the goodness they find within themselves and identify that goodness as coming from, indeed being, God present in them. Most of them can easily see the good within and from there we can help them become aware of so much goodness around them, in spite of so much evil.

We also find that teaching young people to pray is much easier than might be thought. They can quite readily transfer their new awareness of God present in the goodness around them to being able to talk to that God through their own words, which are most powerful prayers. Some of the most sincere prayers I have heard in my life I have heard in our own Covenant House chapels when kids come together, read parts of Scripture, and pray in their own words, usually begging God to strengthen them, help them to forgive and be forgiven, and to start a new life. Their ready will to depend on God is so evident and so readily brought forth.

It seems to me that faith is indeed dormant in every child, and despite its being harmed by experience, that dormant faith can be fanned into fire. But the rekindling may take a lot of patience and faith in the one who fans the sparks.

ANDRE DUBUS

is the author of the short stories collected in The Times Are Never So Bad, Adultery & Other Choices, Finding a Girl in America, *as well as a book of essays,* Broken Vessels. *His work has appeared in* The New Yorker, Esquire, *and other national magazines.*

In 1996 he published Dancing After Hours. *This collection of stories was published a few years after an accident that left Mr. Dubus wheelchair-bound. One night while stopping to help a motorist on the highway, he was hit by a car; both of his legs were shattered.* Dancing After Hours *received the Rea Award for the Short Story. Mr. Dubus lives in Haverhill, Massachusetts.*

For nearly fifty years I found God in prayer and, I think, most of all the Eucharist. I think I also found God in the gift of writing. When I began writing, as a college undergraduate, I prayed each morning that I would write well, of God and for God, and I still say that prayer. When I was nearly fifty, I was hit by a car and crippled and everything changed: not only every physical act I performed, but the way my soul feels in the world. I lost the illusion I had as a biped; that discipline and will were the sources of a full life. Because I had to, I began surrendering to my life as a cripple, a life given to me by God. I pray more often now, and love God in the Eucharist; but the Eucharist, the physical presence of God, has become evident to me in the mundane. I have come to see life as a gift, and each breath as a sacrament.

In my first year as a cripple, a Jesuit friend and a woman who was my Eucharistic minister told me to read the New Testament. They were right. I read a chapter at breakfast, and a meditation by Mother Teresa, and those feed my soul. I do not know how other people can find God. He has given Himself to me since I was a Catholic boy; now He has given me gratitude, and two years ago, when I was in spiritual pain, He taught me to thank Him for that, too: for being alive, to receive pain.

REV. JOHN MCNAMEE

is pastor of St. Malachy Roman Catholic Church in Philadelphia and author of Diary of a City Priest, Endurance, *and* Clay Vessels, *a book of poems. He has worked as a parish priest for over twenty-five years in poor neighborhoods in North Philadelphia.*

Philosopher Gabriel Marcel said that the believer and unbeliever can communicate only when the believer reveals the strains of unbelief in himself. We are all Saint Peter walking on the water: Believing, he walks the waves; unbelieving, he sinks into them. Faith and unfaith together in the same person at the same time. A venerable theology helps me very much here: The will nudges the intellect where the mind would not go for want of clarity or evidence. That nudge is called grace by the scholastics. We are all Cardinal Newman in a dreary Victorian library coming to full faith by turning the pages of early Church Fathers to discover a way "commending itself." Even unbeliever Freud had such a secular hope that in the welter of human emotions the fragile thread of reason could be grasped and followed. *Intellectus quaerens fidem*: understanding in search of faith. Our task is paying attention. What we find is indeed a mystery of grace.

OWEN GINGERICH

is a senior astronomer at the Smithsonian Astrophysical Observatory and professor of astronomy and of the history of science at Harvard University, in Cambridge, Massachusetts. Professor Gingerich is the co-author of two successive standard models for the solar atmosphere, the first to take into account rocket and satellite observations.

In addition to The Album of Science: The Physical Sciences in the Twentieth Century, *Professor Gingerich has edited, translated, or written nineteen other books, and has published over 400 technical, educational, and scholarly articles and reviews. He is also a leading authority on the 17th-century German astronomer Johannes Kepler and on Nicholas Copernicus, the 16th-century cosmologist who proposed the heliocentric system. In recognition of his work on Copernicus, he was awarded Poland's Order of Merit, and, more recently, Asteroid 2685=1980CK was named "Gingerich" in his honor.*

During the past decade, Professor Gingerich has written extensively on science and theology, and is a consultant at the Center for Theological Inquiry in Princeton, New Jersey. He and his wife, Miriam, are enthusiastic travelers, photographers, and rare book and shell collectors.

I passionately believe that the universe has purpose, that it reflects the intentions of a designing superintelligence, and that we as self-conscious and inquiring beings play a fundamental role in the meaning of the universe.

As a scientist who contemplates the universe with this perspective, I am fascinated by the many astonishing features of our world that make intelligent life possible. As a teenager I was amazed to learn that water, unlike the vast majority of substances, expands when it freezes, so that ice floats on water. Without this remarkable property the earth's oceans would freeze from the bottom up, and it would be well nigh impossible to thaw them out again. Perpetually frozen oceans would have severe negative consequences for life on this planet. Eventually I learned that this was only one of several remarkable properties of water that make it uniquely relevant for the existence of life in the universe.

As a practicing astrophysicist, I was awed to learn about the internal energy levels of the carbon nucleus, which allow the relatively easy formation of carbon in the cores of evolving giant stars. Had the energy level in the carbon atom been four percent lower, there would essentially be no carbon. Had the comparable level in the oxygen atom been only half a percent higher, virtually all of the carbon would have been converted to oxygen. This delicate balance guarantees that a great deal of carbon will be produced, enough to make it the fourth most abundant element in the cosmos. Without that high carbon abundance, essential for organic chemistry, neither you nor I would be here right now.

The famous astronomer Fred Hoyle is reported to have said that nothing has shaken his atheism as much as this discovery about the energy structure of the carbon and oxygen nuclei. I have never asked him about that, but the answer is fairly clear from what he once wrote in the Cal Tech alumni magazine:

> Would you not say to yourself, "Some supercalculating intellect must have designed the properties of the carbon atom, otherwise the chance of my finding such an atom through the blind forces of nature would be utterly minuscule?" Of course you would.... The numbers one calculates from the facts seem to me so overwhelming as to put this conclusion almost beyond question.

The physical nature of water and the structure of carbon and oxygen nuclei are but a few of the "design" features of the physical world that lead me to believe that the universe was deliberately planned and constructed to make self-conscious, reflective life possible. But herein lies a dilemma. Impressive as these evidences are to me, I know they fall short of the logical persuasion that might convince a skeptic. From these magnificent facts about the universe there seems no way to *prove* that a designing hand was at work. A skeptic can simply say, "Yes, it's a seemingly remarkable coincidence, but that's how it has to be; if the universe were any other way, we wouldn't be here to contemplate it, and that's that."

But this is only half of my dilemma. Even if I could persuade the skeptic that there must be a superintelligent Creator, then where would we be? Looking at the vastness and complexity of the universe, we would end up with a God of very large numbers, a God worthy of awesome respect if he/she/it was still around, but hardly a God worthy of committed devotion.

As I cogitated the challenge of explaining how to find God, I took a walk around the suburb of Columbus, Ohio, where I was visiting. Suddenly, I came upon three words permanently scratched into the sidewalk when the cement was still wet: "Jesus loves you." I recoiled at the simplistic triteness of the statement, a popular slogan as drained of meaning as the "In God We Trust" emblazoned on our currency. And yet, I realized, behind the worn mottos there are profound truths.

If a Creator is actually and actively interested in Creation, the only method of communication is through human thinking or a human example. Divine knowledge comes through prophets of all ages—men and women of thought and action. Just because our understanding of God comes from thinking about God as we observe the universe and our fellow creatures doesn't mean the results are invalid, any more than our humanly constructed scientific worldview is untrue. What validates these constructions, based on the finite limitations of human language, is the role of society. "And this is my prayer," Paul wrote to the Philippians, "that your love may grow ever richer in knowledge and insight of every kind, and may thus bring you the gift of true discrimination." True discrimination is forged through a community of believers.

I am happy to be a part of a community of faith that finds a role model and an understanding of the nature of God via a man who lived nearly two thousand years ago. There were no clocks or televisions or airplanes then, but much of the bigotry and hatred and terror we know all too well today was the same in the first century A.D. Jesus showed a loving, sacrificial way of dealing with those realities of human existence. I am sure God is revealed in many ways to many people, but this unique model has a great deal to say to us today.

In particular, our increased understanding of the universe in which we live has brought us enormously increased responsibilities, because we now truly hold the power to destroy ourselves. I have often stood on the lecture platform discussing the integrity of the great tapestry of science, how rational humankind can fill in the details of the working out of God's incredible design. For me, the coherency of my own view demands a step further, toward accepting something even more mind-boggling than cosmology or the evolution of intelligent life on earth: God has given us a demonstration of his sacrificial love in the life and death of Jesus Christ. Finding this loving aspect of God is more vital today than it ever was. It means going beyond a Creator

God of large numbers. But unless we can see beyond individual or ethnic greed or selfishness to Christ's sacrificial life and love, I believe that the human race is headed toward nuclear or ecological suicide.

When the psalmist asked, "What is Man, that Thou art mindful of him?" I would answer that as contemplative beings created in the image of God with attributes of creativity, conscience, and self-consciousness, we are central to the purposes of the cosmos. For me faith is not blind faith, but trust. And I trust that the selfish suicide of the human race is not an intended part of the purposefulness of Creation!

MARTIN E. MARTY

is the Fairfax M. Cone Distinguished Professor at the Divinity School of the University of Chicago and senior editor of The Christian Century *magazine. He has written extensively on the place of religion in the United States, and his book* Righteous Empire *received the National Book Award in 1970. Professor Marty, an ordained Lutheran minister, is also the co-editor of* Fundamentalism Observed, *and author of numerous other books, including* Modern American Religion *and* Modern American Protestantism and Its World.

Turn it around: How does God find me? If God is, but is ineffable, beyond beyondness, self-contained, forget it. Then God is unfindable. Rather than seek God, eat pomegranates, shoot pool, listen to Scarlatti, munch almonds, watch fireflies, visit the Andes. If God is, and is ineffable, beyond the gods but still relational, remember it. Then God is findable. While seeking God, eat pomegranates, etc....

God being ineffable is not sufficient for your search. Effable: "that which can be expressed or described in words." "God is addressed, not expressed," says Martin Buber. But address involves a mixture of postures, gestures, stances, and uses of words. "I" meets "Thou," the "Other," the "Different," and, on occasion, despite doubts and suspicions, disappointments and setbacks, mixed signals and unclear signs, one responds with a "Yes," as in "Yes, God."

"How do I find God?" Bum Steer Number One: Find God as yourself and yourself as God; find God in yourself and yourself in God. No. You know yourself well enough to know the specters and the shadows, the uncontrollable will and intractable desire to cling to the old, that haunt you and hold you back. Find God as yourself or in yourself and you will soon get bored with what you've found.

"How do I find God?" Bum Steer Number Two: Find God as energy, connections, nature. No. You know too much about mere chaos, contingency, tarantulas, and earthquakes to count on finding God immediately there.

"How do I find God?" Certainly by beginning with a sense of wonder and being ready for awe. God may cause you to be "surprised by joy." But it may take billions of particulars, including affirmations, recognitions of Christ in the homeless, readings of Scripture, experiences of friendships, transcendings of despair, for this surprise to work its way, to elicit awe from you.

"How do I find God?" The God who is addressed and addresses effably speaks most clearly when words come into play: "Let there be light." "Little children, love one another!" "Christ is risen." That light can dawn in the heart and be in you so, *then*, yes God is "in you." That love can be formed with Christ in the heart and then there are energies and connections with the surrounding universe(s). Yes, *then* God is "around" you. "How do I find God?" By listening closely and, with suspicion momentarily suppressed, by responding. Awe-full, isn't it?

REV. AVERY DULLES, S.J.,

is the Lawrence J. McGinley Professor of Theology at Fordham University in Bronx, New York, and Professor Emeritus at the Catholic University of America. He is past president of both the Catholic Theological Society of America and the American Theological Society.

Father Dulles joined the Society of Jesus in 1946, after serving four years in the U.S. Naval Reserve and receiving France's Croix de Guerre. *He has written extensively on ecclesiology, Catholic doctrine, and the thought of Pope John Paul II. He is the author of hundreds of scholarly articles, as well as seventeen books, including the influential* Models of the Church *and, more recently,* The Assurance of Things Hoped For: A Theology of Christian Faith.

Each story of finding God is different. Individual converts bring to the process all that they have and are: their abilities, temperament, previous experiences and encounters, expectations, desires, and anxieties. There is no common rule.

My own approach to faith was in some degree philosophical. If I were asked to name the critical turning point, I would say that it was the tension between the dictates of virtue and of self-interest. Plato's *Dialogues* convinced me that it would be unacceptable to pursue one's apparent advantage at the expense of what is objectively right and just, and that no one can be made worse by upright conduct. The obligation to do good and avoid evil, I reasoned, must have its source from above, in a higher personal being. An obligation that is absolute (as that obligation evidently is) must have its source in an absolute personal being, i.e., in God. And if we cannot be injured by right conduct, there must be a future life. The One to whom we are accountable must control our ultimate destiny and must know us through and through. I began to consider that we are living always in the presence of a personal being who is Creator, Lawgiver, Judge, and Rewarder. Only after I had come to this conclusion did I begin to recognize the force of other proofs of the existence of God, such as the cosmological argument and the argument from design.

These ruminations gave me the background for finding in the New Testament a luminous revelation of our Creator and Savior, which both fulfilled and surpassed the intimations of philosophy. My personal synthesis of Platonic ethics and biblical faith was deepened and confirmed by works such as the *Confessions* of Saint Augustine. Studies in European history and the reading of dozens of modern authors, together with some visits to Catholic churches, gradually led me to Catholicism.

In answer to your question, then, I would say that the search for God can appropriately begin from a reflection on the voice of conscience. Anyone who experiences the fact of moral obligation has the makings of a belief in God and has the prerequisites for hearing God's word fruitfully. But the hearing of that word will not result in faith unless it is accompanied by prayer. "If you then, who are evil, know how to give good gifts to your children, how much more will the heavenly Father give the Holy Spirit to those who ask him!" (Luke 11:13).

Theologically, it is correct to say that the very desire to find God is evidence that God is drawing us to himself. To find him, in the last analysis, is to be found by him.

Jacque Braman,

a thirty-five-year-old newlywed, has been active in a variety of Protestant churches. Raised in a United Methodist church in Libertyville, Illinois, she attended a Presbyterian church in college, and a non-denominational Bible church after graduation. "I had a friend in college who used to take me to Catholic Masses, too," she remembers. "Palm Sunday was his favorite because of the free palm branches." Later Jacque joined a large charismatic Episcopal church while living in Washington, D.C., where she worked for thirteen years as an information systems analyst. At that church Jacque taught Sunday school, volunteered in feeding programs for homeless families, and also led Bible study groups.

After being married Jacque and her husband, Paul, a systems analyst, moved to Ankeny, Iowa. The move provided a good opportunity for a career change as well, and Jacque is now studying to become a secondary math teacher. During her free time she works from home as an independent computer programming consultant. Jacque and Paul are now members of a small and very new congregation of the Open Bible church. "They are such a new denomination," says Jacque, "that I hadn't heard of them until we moved to Iowa."

How can I find God? I've asked this question myself at times, though not because I have never found him, but rather because at times I feel like I've lost contact. You could say that I first found God as a child. But since I wasn't really looking for him it would be more accurate to say that God found me.

I was raised in the church, went to Sunday school every week, learned all the Bible stories, and pretty much accepted them as truth. After all, I had no reason not to believe. Then God, one night as I was riding in the car, gave me some tangible proof.

It was a peaceful evening. My mom and brother and sister and I were on our way to a high school basketball game that my dad was coaching. It was quiet in the car. The others may have been talking some, but not to me. I was just looking out the window at the still night, enjoying the stars, and the street lights, and happy to be on my way to the game. Then a strange thing started to happen. The happiness that I was feeling grew deeper and richer and fuller, and completely overwhelmed me, even though I still felt quiet and peaceful. Then I noticed that tears were rolling down my cheeks. This was really weird. I double checked: No, I wasn't sad. I had a huge grin plastered on my face, one that was beyond my ability to remove, try as I might. It reminded me of a story we had read in school, in which a pioneer woman was so touched by something that her children had done for her that she cried tears of joy. I thought it was the stupidest thing I had ever heard! People don't cry when they are happy, I remember thinking, they cry when they are sad. Yet here I was, tears streaming down my face, just like the woman in the book.

Then I understood. This was how full joy could be. This was a joy that comes only from God. I relished the moment, immersed in joy, filled with thankfulness and contentment. I shared my thoughts with God in silent prayer, and knew he was right there with me.

On subsequent nights, God would play a sort of enjoyable "game" with me. As I lay in bed ready for sleep, God would revisit me with that amazing joy. He would put a great big grin on my face, and I would try my hardest to remove it, but I just couldn't. And every time it happened, I just knew that it was God, and I thought it was so cool that God would come to me like this.

Over time God began to play less and less frequently. Sometimes weeks, or even months, would go by without the tangible assurance of his presence. It got to the point where the game became a vague memory, and I started to doubt whether it had ever happened at all. I would doubt God's presence, his love, his personal concern for my life, even his reality. Was it all just make-believe? Wishful thinking? If I couldn't find him when I searched for him, what was the point of believing? I longed for the confidence that I once had.

After what seemed like a very long time, perhaps a year or more, God surprised me again with his joy. It was as I was lying in bed, just like before. The reality of his presence was overwhelming, and all of my doubts evaporated in an instance, and I knew in the very depths of my being that God was there with me. This time I prayed that he would never let me forget the absolute certainty that I felt at that moment. I simply knew, beyond all reason, logic, or evidence, that God was real and that he was with me. And I also knew that I would need to remember, because this was the last time he might prove himself to me in this way.

Since then, there have been many times when God has seemed silent, though I have searched for him and cried out to him with all my heart. I've felt lost and alone, desperate for the God that other people would say was there to comfort them in their grief and anguish, but yet seemed so elusive to me. And when I've cried all my tears and exhausted all my emotions, and still feel as far away from God as ever, he answers my prayer, and I remember. I remember the absolute certainty with which I knew, on that night so long ago, that God was real and that he was with me. And I know that it is still true, that he is still there, hearing my prayers and watching over me, even though I cannot feel him and do not know how I will make it through tomorrow.

Fortunately, the times of despair do not last forever. When things are going well, it's easier to believe in God than when life is hard. But God wants us to have faith at all times. He will reveal himself to us as we need, but there will be times when he requires us to seek him and persevere in faith. God promises that we will find him when we seek him with all our hearts. Tell God all your thoughts and concerns in prayer. Read about him in the Bible. Ask those who claim to know God to tell you more about him. Don't let up in your search until you find him. Quiet your soul and wait for him. In his time, God will reveal himself to you. You have his word on it:

> You call upon me and come and pray to me, and I will hear you. When you search for me, you will find me; if you seek me with all your heart, I will let you find me, says the LORD (Jeremiah 29:12–14).

Rev. Holly Lyman Antolini

serves as Vicar of the Episcopal Mission of St. Brendan-the-Navigator, which meets in St. Mary's Star-of-the-Sea Catholic Church in Stonington, Maine. Raised as an agnostic, Ms. Antolini was baptized in 1980 and ordained to the priesthood in 1991.

Rev. Antolini, a 1974 graduate of Yale University, had spent a number of years with Sunset Magazines, *writing cookbooks and books on solar heating. Her participation in a local church gradually drew her into Christianity. "I'd been singing in the choir," she remembers, "and eventually I got tired of being left out of communion." She is married to Dr. Anthony Antolini, a Slavic linguistics scholar and choral director at Bowdoin College, and has two daughters, ages eleven and fourteen. In addition to her parochial service, she works with the Committee on Indian Relations of the Episcopal Diocese of Maine, and serves on her local school board. In each of these capacities, as well as in cultivating her extensive vegetable garden, Rev. Antolini says, "I find myself in communion with God."*

For those of us imbued with the skepticism of modern science, it is no longer possible simply to "take the Bible's word for it" that God exists, or that Jesus is God's Son. If you're coming to me wondering how to find God, I will not presume to insist that you base your relationship with God on an eternal authority imposed by tradition or by figures endowed with authority by an institution. Such an insistence simply won't hold up against the "Question authority!" mood of our time.

Instead I ask you to seek God in *eucharist*, which is Greek for "thanksgiving," and which also is the word we use in the Episcopal Church for the central worship service of each week, the Holy Eucharist. Seek God in both these senses: seek God in the Holy Eucharist, at least weekly. And seek God by cultivating a spirit of thanksgiving for every jot and tittle—even the painful ones—of your life, for what these details can teach you of God, and as gifts of God's mysterious providence. These two paths proceed together, as here in Maine "Route 3" can also be "Route 32." Not only can you find God on this dual path; God can find you.

There are many ways for you and God to find each other. A Buddhist or a Taoist might send you on other paths. But I am an Episcopalian Christian, and that's why I suggest that a good place to start looking for God is by becoming part of a eucharistic community: a community of people who support each other to awaken to gratitude, day by day and week by week, by coming together in a service of holy thanksgiving, which centers on the self-offering gift of Jesus Christ.

In the first half of any service of Holy Eucharist, called the Ministry of the Word, you join a great and ancient conversation about how to commune with God. You find your own experience coming into conversation with the experiences of God related in the Bible, just as the different writers and storytellers whose works make up the Bible converse with each other in that complex collection of Scripture, bringing their many different perspectives to bear on the search for God. You also bring your own experience into conversation with figures and traditions from 4,000 years of Judeo-Christian history of God's relationship with God's people and the whole of creation. In addition, you and the other seekers in the community share with each other experiences of God's self-revelation in the particulars of your lives. This great conversation is a communion in itself: a communion of many insights. But it takes commitment and time and a willingness on your part to be both lost and found for it to become your communion with God.

Nevertheless, over time, if the voices in this conversation speak to you as they have spoken to me, reaching into my life and drawing me closer to God, they will begin to tell you that every aspect of your life is pregnant with meaning and sacred, created and sustained in God's love. Just as Mary became pregnant with Jesus—with God—so every aspect of your life can reveal God to you. If you listen attentively to these voices, if you let the Spirit of God begin to breathe its insights into you, you will start looking for God's hand at work in the everyday events of your life, wherever you find truth, or beauty, or justice, or forgiveness increasing. And not only your human relationships will start to reveal God and God's gifts to you, but other relationships as well, relationships with the natural world. The clearer God's caring presence in your life, the greater your gratitude will grow. The greater your gratitude, the more you will be drawn to imitate God's loving care as Jesus Christ reveals it to us.

This is because as the conversation in the eucharistic community—the Ministry of the Word—draws you closer to God, reaching out and penetrating every aspect of your life, it also draws you closer and closer to the heart of the service of the Holy Eucharist—its second half—which is called the "Holy Communion." This part of the service moves into prayer and almost beyond words. Here we partake of bread broken and wine poured out to symbolize Jesus' willingness to offer his whole life up for love of us all on the Cross. In partaking of this bread and wine, we commune with God mysteriously, so deeply that we literally become part of Christ, part of Christ's spirit of self-offering.

But be warned: The way to God as I know it is full of joy, but it is also a Way of the Cross. The Holy Communion commemorates how Jesus allowed himself to be crucified for his insistence on acting only out of love for God and God's creation, and not out of self-preservation. In so doing, and in our participation in the commemoration, this Spirit of compassion and generosity is awakened in us and calls us out of our own anxious self-seeking. In communion, we are driven to offer ourselves alongside Jesus to make God's love and abundance known in the places where, because of injustice or neglect or illness or abuse or tragedy of any kind, people are imprisoned in alienation and scarcity. Such a self-offering is likely to involve us in the pain and suffering of others to an extraordinary degree. It will even lead some of us literally to death at the hands of those who will not tolerate the perceived threat to their identity, as it led Jesus. But as Paul says in his Letter to the Romans, "If we have died with Christ, we believe that we will also live with him." The Way of the Cross is the way to life lived without reserve, life lived in complete thanksgiving, life in its fullest: communion with God.

HON. PAUL SIMON

served as United States Senator from Illinois from 1984 to 1997. In 1987 to 1988, he sought the Democratic nomination for president. During his time in the Senate, Mr. Simon served on the Budget, Labor and Human Resources, Judiciary, and Indian Affairs Committees, and authored major education and job-training initiatives.

Prior to his career in government service, Mr. Simon served two years (1951-1953) in the U.S. Army and was assigned to the Counter-Intelligence Corps as a special agent along the Iron Curtain in Europe. Beginning in 1954, he served fourteen years in the Illinois State Legislature. Mr. Simon holds thirty-nine honorary degrees and has written or co-written fifteen books, including Lincoln's Preparation for Greatness, A Hungry World, *and, with his wife, Jeanne Hurley Simon,* Protestant-Catholic Marriages Can Succeed.

The unknown will always exceed the known in any thoughtful person's reach for the ultimate realities. We are limited in that search by our perception of reality.

In a psychology class at Dana College in Nebraska, the instructor assigned each of us to go to our dormitory washrooms, which in those days constituted one large room for an entire floor, and put hot water in one small sink, cold water in another, and a blend of hot and cold in the third. "Put one hand in the hot water, one hand in the cold water, and after thirty seconds, put both hands in the mixed water," he instructed us. When we did that, one hand told our brain that the mixed water was cold, the other that it was warm. "Which hand is correct?" he asked us.

All of us make judgments on the basis of our experiences. Until her death, my marvelous mother-in-law believed that Neil Armstrong did not walk on the moon, that it was all a Hollywood set. Most of us found the moon landing beyond anything we had imagined.

I believe that the ultimate realities far exceed our ability to ponder man's trip to the moon and are beyond anything we can imagine.

When I see my new grandson, or look at an elephant or a small bug, or stand in awe of a flower or a tree, my sense is that all of this cannot have happened by accident, that there is a Creator. At the same time, I don't believe that someone designed my body's plumbing system in all its infinite complexity, or that the Creator wants a child to be stricken by cancer or adults by Alzheimer's, or for men and women to die of starvation or in war.

There is this vast unknown.

That is where the Danish philosopher Søren Kierkegaard says we must make a "leap of faith." That leap is made to Christianity or Judaism or some other faith, or it is not made. Some leap further than others.

Many have failed to distinguish between faith and arrogance. To see people killed in the name of religion and zealotry; to assume that "our group," however it is defined, has a monopoly on truth and others have no insights, frequently turns me off on organized religion.

But my search continues.

REV. THEODORE M. HESBURGH, C.S.C.,

served as president of the University of Notre Dame in Indiana from 1952 through 1987, and is one of the world's most distinguished educators. In addition to receiving the Medal of Freedom in 1964, the nation's highest civilian honor, he is also the recipient of 130 honorary degrees, the most ever awarded to one person. Over the years, Father Hesburgh, a member of the Congregation of the Holy Cross, has held fifteen Presidential appointments, involving him in many major social issues—civil rights, peaceful uses of atomic energy, Third World development and immigration reform, to name a few.

Today, as president emeritus, Father Hesburgh continues his busy schedule, traveling, lecturing, writing, as well as often presiding over liturgies on campus. His 1990 autobiography God, Country, Notre Dame *became a national bestseller.*

I am sure one finds God in as many ways as there are people, but there are some easy ways to find him, especially in today's world.

I believe that the easiest way to find God is to read the New Testament thoughtfully and meditatively. Here we read about God Himself becoming Man. God gives us many ways of finding Him as we read His words and follow the wonderful life He lived publicly for three years.

One of the most wonderful of the New Testament stories comes when Jesus spoke about how we would be judged at the end of our lives. He simply said that, at that time, God will say to us, “I was hungry and you gave me to eat, I was thirsty and you gave me to drink, I was sick and you cared for me, I was homeless and you took me in, I was naked and you clothed me.”

And then, He said, people would be surprised, and would ask him, “Lord, when did I see You hungry, thirsty, sick, homeless and naked?” His answer was quite clear: “When you did this for one of these my least brethren, you did it for me.”

It seems so simple. The world is full of people who are hungry and thirsty, sick and homeless, as well as naked in so many ways. They all need help, and in helping them, we are not only finding God but serving Him as well. How simple this is.

When I look around at our students at Notre Dame today, and find three-quarters of them serving the poor in a wide variety of ways, I know that they are not only finding God but also serving Him. It is difficult to find anything as simple, but there it is: It is not our idea but God’s, which He told us in such a simple and plain way. It has to be one of the easiest ways of finding God in our very complicated world.

TOM OSBORNE

has been since 1973 the head coach of the University of Nebraska football team, national champions in 1994 and 1995. Mr. Osborne is also active in the Fellowship of Christian Athletes and supports numerous area youth education programs. He has received the Amos Alonzo Stagg Award for coaching excellence and holds the record for most Bowl games after "Bear" Bryant and Joe Paterno. Mr. Osborne lives in Lincoln, Nebraska, with his wife, Nancy, and family.

I would say that an individual needs first to know something about God, and the best place to start is in the Bible. I believe that the Bible reveals more about God than any other source that we could come to.

Second, I believe that it is important that the person attempt to come to know God through prayer. I think an active prayer and meditation that is regular and systematic is very important. It is important to take some time to listen as well as to give prayers of supplication and petition.

I would say that it is important for a person to behave actively in ways toward other people that are consistent with what you know God would have you do as revealed by the Scriptures and your prayer life. As you begin to practice your faith, you will come to know more about God and what He would have you do.

You will encounter God sometimes in other people, sometimes in nature, and sometimes in prayer, meditation and Scripture reading.

MELINDA RUBEN

is a professional educator who has taught in a variety of settings: home, public schools, afternoon religious schools, and a private Jewish day school. Upon graduating from Harvard University with a degree in English and American Literature, she enjoyed a career in publishing and advertising. Next, Melinda spent several years devoted to what she calls "birthing, nursing, and child-rearing."

In 1995 Melinda earned a master's degree in elementary education from Lesley College in Boston. Today, she lives in Sharon, Massachusetts, with her three young children, and teaches fourth-grade children, full time, at a Conservative Jewish day school in Stoughton, Massachusetts. Melinda has also facilitated professional workshops on current issues in education, such as gender sensitivity and special needs, and continues, as she says, "to read voraciously."

I believe that anyone motivated to ask the question of how to find God has already begun. Faith in God is a lifelong process of searching, learning, and acting—not some magical product. And faith is a private license, easily revoked by reason, experience and doubt—not a framed credential.

My response to the search for God is rooted in personal and professional experiences, and is a synthesis of traditional Jewish and existential theories. My own religious identification has been formed by the demands of education, desperation, affiliation, and generation.

The moments in my life when I felt that I had actually found God are few but clear: When I was eight I had to undergo extensive medical treatment for excruciating, chronic earaches. Angry and sad, I went to my family's rabbi to ask Job's eternal question: "Why, if there is a God, is he allowing me to suffer?" The rabbi's answer was less important than his very presence and scholarship, which gave me hope that God existed.

As a student, I pursued a Jewish education along with my secular studies. At one point during my time at Hebrew College I participated in a summer study program in Israel. Our group camped in the desert and climbed what was believed to be Mount Sinai. There, at age fifteen, I found God. I stood atop the mountain, prayed with my friends, and felt as if God were giving me the Torah as a personal gift.

Later, during my late teens and twenties, I became rebellious, Godless. But when I married, separation from my parents and my connection to my husband turned me once again toward God. I found God during my synagogue wedding as I signed the *Ketubah* (the Jewish wedding contract) in a private room and walked down the aisle on a carpet of tradition. The subsequent births of my three children were celebrated by my sons' ritual circumcisions and my daughter's Hebrew naming ceremony. These are the times that I knew God would stay. I began to feel that the responsibility of my Jewish education committed me to transmit that tradition to my children. In doing so, I felt, in all humility, that I was fulfilling the commandment of Deuteronomy 6:7: "You shall teach them diligently to your children."

What does this ordinary biography offer to you who are trying to find God? A heartfelt message of hope. A message that despair, pain, and doubt may lead you to the comfort of God. A message that education will teach you the value of God. A message that the life cycle events of marriage, birth, and even death, will oblige you to find God.

Too vague or irrelevant? OK, then I'll offer you another road...

Judaism depends on a tripod of ritual and prayer (observance), *mitzvot* and deeds (ethical behavior), and Torah (study). Try one. Read a prayer. Say the *Shema* one morning. Attend a synagogue service. Visit the sick. Donate to a food pantry or charity. Make a *Pesach Seder*. Read the Torah. Learn Hebrew. Attend a seminar. Affix a *mezuzah* to your doorpost. Eat a kosher meal. Dance at a Jewish wedding. Light the Sabbath candles. Depending on your personality and lifestyle, one ritual, one deed, and one Torah passage may lead to another. And you're on your way.

Another effective route for those in search of God is literally one of travel. Visit Israel. The beauty of the land, the spirit of the people, the enlivenment of the Bible are all powerful connectors to God, for Jews as well as Christians and Muslims.

Too impractical? Then go to a local synagogue or church or mosque. Visit an affiliated community center.

Oh, you're still skeptical. You want a more intellectual or theoretical guide? The writings of theologian Martin Buber stress that in Judaism teaching is inseparable from doing. He compares the Greek and Mosaic understanding of knowledge: *sophia* and *hokmah*. *Sophia* is a closed realm of thought where knowledge is attained for its own sake, and virtue is cognition. In contrast, *hokmah* is the unity of teaching and life wherein cognition is never enough. "What counts," wrote Buber "is...to know what one knows, and to believe what one believes, so directly that it can be translated into the life one lives....The teachings cannot be severed from the deed, but neither can the deed be severed from the teachings!"

Too matronizing or sermonizing? Then let's try again. I would also recommend the concept of *teshuvah*, or repentance, as an alternate ladder to God.

In Hebrew, *teshuvah* means an answering or returning. "At its most sweeping *teshuvah* involves a complete overhaul of priorities—replacing our preoccupation with our own needs, perspectives, and concerns with those of God's," writes Bradley S. Artson in his book, *It's a Mitzvah*.

Still too abstract? OK, here's a concrete, step-by-step guide to approaching God through the model of *teshuvah*. Although *Rosh Hashanah* (the Jewish New Year) is traditionally a period of introspection, *teshuvah* is not limited to any particular time. You may be ready now if you feel the need to balance your belief in human goodness with your awareness of fallibility. Try these few steps, outlined by medieval rabbis: Recognize that an action is wrong, separate the action from the doer, confess the act by speaking, reconcile yourself with the wronged party, make restitution by performing an act to balance the error, and, finally, resolve to strive for improvement and commit not to repeat the offense.

Although I don't profess to be a theological expert, I do propose a variety of means to help you search for God. Such a search, I assume, stems from a very real, human need to find meaning in life. Ritual, prayer, study, travel, children, family, and introspection are all possible ways to God. Enjoy each for its own sake and perhaps, along one path, you will find that for which you are searching.

REV. LEO O'DONOVAN, S.J.,

is president of Georgetown University in Washington, D.C. Prior to his work at Georgetown, Father O'Donovan, a member of the Society of Jesus, taught at the Weston Jesuit School of Theology in Cambridge, Massachusetts. He is the editor of A World of Grace, *an anthology of writings on the Catholic theologian Karl Rahner.*

The paradox has only grown deeper for me in life's course, namely, that seeking God always precedes and supports and follows any sense of "finding." I remember so well first hearing Ignatius of Loyola's marvelous counsel to find God in all things. At the time, it seemed both self-evidently true and a profound blessing. But gradually, by experiencing again and again the universality of Christ's cross, the hazard and anguish of the process has become more clear. "I greet Him the days I meet Him," wrote Gerard Manley Hopkins, "and bless when I understand." And what we understand best in the darkness, far beyond all our striving and reaching, is how much more profoundly God is in search of us and, "with ah! bright wings" bent on finding us.

Anthony Scola,

of Hindman, Kentucky, describes himself as a "Catholic Quaker." The description is apt. Anthony, a Roman Catholic with a master's degree in English linguistics from Notre Dame and another in Spanish literature from the University of Kentucky, is currently in his fourth year of volunteer service with the Mennonite Central Committee. He and his wife, Margaret, recently spent two years teaching in Khartoum, Sudan, and two in Appalachia. They have recently moved to Asunción, Paraguay, to take up another teaching assignment.

Anthony and his wife have raised foster children and are active in both Quaker and Catholic activities and organizations. Both were members of Catholic religious orders before their marriage in 1976.

Whatever or wherever God is, we learn only gradually through our daily life. A cornerstone of Quaker belief is that we find the "that of God" in everyone. This means that all people (and by extension, all creation) somehow reflect the presence of God. If we keep this idea in our consciousness, it will affect how we view other people and, consequently, how we imagine God to be. For example, we've all had the experience of recognizing some profound wisdom coming from a most unexpected source. When someone disagrees with me, challenges me, or offends me, I can either remain open to whatever message God is giving me within that person or ignore it. But I had better pay attention if I honestly want to see God in that moment.

I recently saw a sign in front of a church reading: "Listen to the Word of God!" This made me think of the many ways that God speaks the word to us. The person who placed the sign there no doubt was referring specifically to the Scriptures, but I think that is too limited a source. After all, God speaks to us constantly, if only we take time to listen. When we talk with others, read books, observe nature or reflect on life, God speaks to us. The truth of God is all around us, we just have to keep looking and listening.

We can learn to see and hear more than we ordinarily do if we periodically close our eyes and ears to the commotion around us. The many activities of daily life, whether as prosaic as preparing supper or as sublime as discovering the medical cure of the century, amount to nothing unless we reflect on them, trying to find out what God has to say to us through such activity. I think it is fruitful to maintain an interplay, a healthy tension, between action and reflection.

For those who regard themselves as seekers (which, by the way, was an early name for the Quakers), another dimension of the quest for God is to trust oneself. If we are truly open and sincere in our search, our body, mind, and spirit will not lead us far afield. Human nature is not self-destructive, it develops for its own good. And so we can trust our gut that we are moving not only toward survival but also toward positive development. That's a pretty optimistic view, I admit. It doesn't mean that we should close our eyes to the tragedy and suffering in our world, it only means that even the negative side of life can be an avenue to God. We take it all—joy, pain, comfort, anguish—and ask ourselves how God speaks to us at this moment. However, in any given experience God does not necessarily speak to you and me in the same way. So there is no single "correct" interpretation suitable to every person.

If there is one word to describe my feelings about God, it is *gratitude*. I find myself suffused with an acute and sometimes overwhelming sense of gratitude for all that is my life. We are surrounded with growth, change, and opportunity, all of which make the journey exciting. How fortunate to be engaged in the quest!

If we don't know God with certainty, then we need to remain open to whatever comes along in the life that we *do* know in order to learn about God. Only when we embrace the world we live in can we accept God with love and awe and reverence.

KATHLEEN NORRIS,

an award-winning poet, is the author of Dakota: A Spiritual Geography *and* The Cloister Walk. *Her five books of poetry include the recent* Little Girls in Church.

Ms. Norris was born in Washington, D.C., and attended high school in Honolulu, but spent most of her childhood summers in Lemmon, South Dakota. In 1971, after graduating from Bennington College in Vermont and working in New York City, she published her first volume of poetry, Falling Off. *Shortly afterward, she returned to her grandparents' house in South Dakota. Today, Ms. Norris lives there with her husband, David Dwyer, a poet.*

Though Ms. Norris comes from what she calls a "completely Protestant background," she has also been since 1986 an oblate (lay associate) of Assumption Abbey, a Benedictine monastery in North Dakota. Her experiences as an oblate formed the basis for The Cloister Walk.

First of all, relax, and be assured that God is also seeking you.

During the many years when I would have described my religion as "nothing," I was annoyed to find that I had a strong emotional response to the few church services I did attend, usually weddings or funerals. I now see that my tears, whether occasioned by anger, joy, nostalgia, or a mixture of all three, were a means God was using to stay in touch. When I discovered "the gift of tears" in early monastic stories, I realized that my unsettling responses to worship, to singing hymns, and hearing the Word of God, had a place in the Christian tradition. In my tears were the seeds of conversion.

Now I find God most readily in communal worship, and in the words of Scripture. I believe that the Bible witnesses to a God who desires an intimate relationship with us. But having spent so many years as an outsider looking in on the Christian religion, I know how strange and impenetrable it can seem. I was educated to believe that religion was something for the gullible, maybe grandmothers and small children. But not for the intellectually respectable. It has helped me to learn that at its root, the word "believe" means not merely an assent of the mind, but "to give one's heart to." Conversely, what we give our hearts to is what we believe. For many of us, including myself, all too often this means that we believe only in ourselves—our work, our plans, our ideas. Ours is an enormously anxious and self-conscious age, and even our religious impulses are often channeled into accomplishments: so many good deeds done, workshops attended, techniques of prayer mastered. Fortunately, because God is not an idea but essential reality, we can be liberated from the trap of self-absorption. But relaxing is important, letting go so that others might reveal God to us. Simply paying close attention to the ways in which we are called to respond to other people might be a place to begin.

In the story of Emmaus, Jesus leads the disciples to discover him both in the Scriptures and in the act of offering hospitality to a stranger. I interpret this to mean that God seeks us through the stranger, and while this means allowing people I think I know well—my husband of twenty years, for example—to be a stranger, his own mysterious self that I will never fully comprehend, it also means being willing to be fully present to the strangers I meet.

I have had to travel a great deal in recent months, and have been astonished at the many ways in which God's presence has been mediated through other people. One day as I was boarding an airplane a businessman noticed that my bracelet had dropped to the floor. He picked it up and handed it to me without a word. I thanked him and never saw him again. The coral bracelet, not valuable in monetary terms, is one that my husband gave me, and I would hate to lose it. I went into the airplane toilet and cried; all my resentment of the travel that was keeping me apart from my husband came out, as did my joy at the mystery of our marriage, of being so united that even apart, we feel like "one flesh." I had just been powerfully reminded, in a busy week in which it seemed imperative to have things "under control," that grace is nothing I can obtain for myself. I was poor and needy, after all, and had not realized how thirsty I was for a bit of mercy, a simple act of kindness.

On another day, I had to put my own neediness aside and listen to a stressed-out woman, hired to pick me up at the airport, who talked incessantly about the fires and gruesome casualties caused by the last fatal crash at the airport where I'd just landed, and where I would be taking off again the next day. She also told stories about blowouts and brake failures she'd had in the car I was riding in on a busy freeway, at sixty miles an hour. Just listen, I told myself, and then I heard the fear underlying everything she said; I began to comprehend that things were not well with her husband's business, and with the marriage itself. Setting aside my own fears, I was able to remember compassion.

On another day I approached an airport taxi stand where two drivers were deep in conversation in a language that sounded like Russian. Bone-weary, and longing for a quiet ride to my hotel and a nap, as the cab left the airport I was just curious enough to venture an innocuous remark about the weather. I asked the driver if there had been recent hailstorms in the vicinity and he said no, but had I ever read the accounts in medieval Italian literature of hailstorms so violent that they killed eleven cattle and sometimes people on pilgrimage? I sat up, realizing that this was a man who was desperate to talk about literature. I asked him if he had ever read Robert Louis Stevenson's *Travels with a Donkey in the Cevennes*. Of course, he said, and then we tossed the names of favorite authors back and forth: Austen, Dickens, Proust, Twain. I encouraged him to read Richard Wilbur, a poet he had not heard of. He asked me, "How is it that so many Americans don't know their own literature, let alone Pushkin?" and I told him it was a long story. He had been a teacher in Belorussia, he said, and longed to teach again. When I named some of the Russian writers I had read in English translation—Akhmatova, Bulgakov, Mandelstam—he began to recite long passages in Russian, so that I could hear the beauty of the language. He was glad to be speaking poetry in his native tongue. And I was glad to be hearing poetry. Even in a language I didn't know, its music was balm for my soul.

Such is God's love in the world, hidden among us. When it breaks forth, it gives us far more than we could have asked for, more than we can imagine. And all that love demands of us is a bit of self-forgetfulness. As Thomas Merton once said, "because we love, God is present."

VERY REV. PETER-HANS KOLVENBACH, S.J.,

is superior general of the Society of Jesus, and resides in Rome. Prior to his election as superior general, Father Kolvenbach, a native of the Netherlands, taught linguistics at the Université de Saint Joseph in Beirut, Lebanon and served as the rector of the Pontifical Oriental Institute in Rome.

"You would not be searching for me unless you had already found me," as Pascal suggests. In this sentence, the question posed already contains an answer of a sort. The question brings to mind an experience of a famous abbot in the Middle Ages. I see myself more or less in his story. This abbot used to speak very well, every morning to his monks, on finding God, on searching for God, on encountering God. He carried on until the day on which a monk dared to ask him if he himself had ever encountered God. After a bit of embarrassed silence, the abbot frankly admitted he never had a vision or a one-on-one meeting with God. Nothing surprising about that, since God Himself had said to Moses, "You cannot see my face." (Exodus 33:20). But this very same God taught Moses that he could see His back as He passed across his path. "You will see me pass." And thus, looking back over the length and breadth of his life the abbot could see for himself the passage of God.

For the One, who wishes to write together with each of us

our individual history, comes and abides to live life with us—often despite us. Without these respectful, but definitive passages of God, our life would not now be what it is. In this sense, it is less a matter of searching for God than of allowing oneself to be found by Him in all of life's situations, where He does not cease to pass and where he allows Himself to be recognized once He has really passed: "You will see my back."

Ron

wrote his response from inside his prison cell in the Suffolk County House of Correction in Boston. His life story is included in this open and honest essay.

My name is Ron and I am twenty-nine years old. I am a recovering cocaine addict serving twenty-seven months for grand theft auto and breaking and entering. I am also HIV positive—a direct result of my addiction to cocaine (intravenous drug use). I would like to explain a little about how I came to this point in my life and how I deal with it mentally, spiritually, and physically.

I grew up in a typical dysfunctional family. My mother was an alcoholic/addict. My stepdad was an alcoholic and my grandparents were alcoholics. My biological father, who I did not meet till I was a young teenager, was an alcoholic addict who spent most of his life in prison for manslaughter, bank robberies, and attempted murder.

Even though I grew up in a dysfunctional family, I feel I had a fairly happy childhood. I guess I can say that today because I didn't know anything different.

When I was fourteen years old my stepfather deserted me and my mom. It was at this time my mom decided to introduce me to my biological father. Meeting him was a real experience for me. He introduced me to a totally new life filled with crime, drugs, and violence.

At that point of my life I was very confused about who I was and what direction my life should go in, so I started experimenting with drugs to find the answers. I liked getting high and I quickly graduated from being a recreational user to an abuser, and eventually a stone-cold addict.

Cocaine was my drug of choice; I was always looking for bigger and better ways to get high on it. I started out sniffing it, tried smoking, then someone turned me on to mainlining it with a hypodermic needle. I loved it and became a full-fledged junkie.

I was living on a day-to-day basis, hustling, stealing and carrying on life without a cause or purpose—no world existed outside of my drug life where I lived. There were no hopes of a better future. There were no great memories of yesterday. There was only living for my next high.

How was I to change at this stage of my life? I found it extremely difficult; in fact, I believed I couldn't change. I was just so used to living the lifestyle, I had no idea of there ever being alternatives I could choose from. The only thing I cared about was getting high. I thought my life would end up the same as many others I've known—dead or in prison.

I was right on both accounts: I ended up in prison with a death sentence hanging over my head—because of my intravenous drug use I tested positive for the HIV virus that causes AIDS. I was devastated and knew there was absolutely no way of turning back now.

The next seven years of my life was a dreadful nightmare of drugs, crime, and prisons. I would get out of prison and run myself ragged on a path of self-destruction.

I now look back at those times as closing a chapter in my life and beginning a new one. Eventually, I was forced to face a change. I resisted change as much as I possibly could, and resistance brought nothing but exhaustion and misery. Change was all I had left and I decided not to let my life end at that point.

For me, the change came with the realization that all my self-destructive behaviors and emotions were a call for help from deep down within myself. I feel that by opening my heart to myself I found a new person, a person who can be compassionate, caring, and most of all open-minded with himself. When I became more open-minded a whole new world opened up before my eyes. What I came to understand was that you are capable of change no matter how bad off you think you are.

When I came to prison this time I was tired of the lifestyle I had been living. I wanted to wipe my slate clean. I took advantage of education, recovery, and counseling programs. I found the support in prison to make the necessary changes in my life to be a more caring, open-minded, and productive individual. Now I am taking advantage of every resource I can so that I can make a plan for myself and be successful in my recovery and life when I am released.

I had to face all the hidden lies and deceit that I had been living throughout my life. In the past, I never accepted what I did as wrong or immoral. It was just my way of surviving.

Since re-examining myself I find I am totally accountable for my actions and accept the responsibilities for my actions. It wasn't until I fully accepted what I did that healing could actually begin. I believe it took a miracle for me to change. I see guys in recovery who had been using drugs and doing crime change, and it's a miracle—you see them change completely. You see them start to care about others. You think that if there was hope for that person, if that person can change, then there's hope for me, and you want what they have. You begin to believe and know that there is a greater power directing things because you see that power reveal itself.

For me, finding God is not about reading the Bible or going to church; its about a connection, it's about the way you live your life. It's like there is a bigger plan and your life fits into it.

JON HASSLER

is the author of ten novels, including Staggerford, Grand Opening, Dear James, *and* Rookery Blues. *His novels, set in the familiar environs of small-town Minnesota, often explore the sacredness of human relationships. Mr. Hassler is also professor of English and writer-in-residence at St. John's University in Collegeville, Minnesota.*

I'm no authority, but I suspect that one finds God while looking for something else, much the way a novelist will find that his writing style has coalesced between the lines of his novel while he was absorbed in his plot and characters and scarcely conscious of where he put his commas.

Fifty-five years ago I recall Sister Constance saying that because playing came naturally to children, we served God by playing. What a liberating thing for us to hear! As third-graders, we'd been struggling so hard to memorize the catechism, pray five times a day, and refrain from eating or drinking before Communion that we were led to believe that being good was like picking your way through a minefield. And then to be told that playing was not only fun but pleasing to God—*whew*!

This truth was brought home to me thirty years later, when I began seriously to write novels. At first, I was rather alarmed to discover that the deeper I went into my fiction, the less devoted I became to the rituals of Catholicism. But now after ten novels,

I've stopped being alarmed. Instead, I'm convinced that my writing springs from the same underground current that used to feed my prayer life. I pray much less often, yet I feel involved in a useful mission. I didn't see it coming, I didn't ask for it, but, judging by what I hear from my readers, I seem to have been ordained to scatter my stories among people who enjoy them, value them, and actually seem to *need* them.

Allow me a few examples: "How do you know so much about the soul of an old man?" (This reaction came from an elderly reader of *Simon's Night*). "Yours was the only book my mother wanted to read as she lay dying of cancer. She read until she couldn't hold the book anymore, and then I read to her. She lived until it was done" (*Dear James*). "I'm a Lutheran minister, and now I begin to understand how a Catholic priest tried to handle his impossible vow of celibacy" (*North of Hope*). "I'm a Jew married to a Catholic, and your book has taught me how my husband thinks" (*A Green Journey*).

I can't take credit for any of this. I didn't set out to write informative, consoling works. Each day, sitting down at my desk, I intend simply to tell a story as clearly and gracefully as I can. It must be Providence. It feels like play.

Huston Smith

is a renowned authority on the history of the world's religious traditions. His major work, The World's Religions *(originally published under the title* The Religions of Man), *has been in continuous publication since 1958 and has been translated into fourteen languages. His series of discussions with Bill Moyers,* The Wisdom of Faith with Huston Smith, *was broadcast on PBS for the first time in 1996. He is also the author of* Huston Smith: Essays on World Religions *and* Forgotten Truth: The Perennial Wisdom of Religious Tradition.

Professor Smith, born of missionary parents in China, describes himself as a pilgrim who seeks to experience the spiritual truths of the religions he studies. A Methodist, he practices yoga, prays five times a day as Muslims do, studies Zen Buddhism, and joins his daughter and her Jewish husband in observing the Sabbath. Today Professor Smith lives in Berkeley, California, with his wife, where he is Visiting Professor of Religious Studies at the University of California. He is also the Thomas J. Watson Professor of Religion, as well as Distinguished Professor of Philosophy, Emeritus, at Syracuse University in New York.

It was said of Mark Van Doren, one of the great teachers of our century, that his distinctive talent lay in helping his students discover who they were. The "who" ran a wide gamut. Some became lifelong existentialists, others committed Marxists. Thomas Merton became a Catholic monk.

On his way to that vocation, Merton asked Van Doren how he could become a saint. Van Doren told him to *want* to become one, and that is probably also the best comprehensive directive for finding God. "Seek and ye shall find; knock and it shall be opened to you," is the Christian formulation of the point, but Ramakrishna's was more graphic. He told a story of a disciple who put the question of finding God to his master. The master led him into the river they were standing by, pushed his head under the water, and held it there until the disciple fought his way to the surface for air. "How did it feel, down there?" the master asked. "It was terrible," the student replied; "I felt like I was going to suffocate." "When you want God as much as you then wanted air," the master concluded, "you will find him very quickly."

As I say, longing seems to hold the key, but there is one further suggestion that I shall venture. Somewhere Plotinus makes the obvious but often overlooked point that if you are looking for something it helps to know *where* to look for it. And where we can most effectively look for God depends on our spiritual personality type; which is to say, on what our chief religious aptitude is. Hinduism's four yogas (four paths to the divine) now belong to the world, and its classification of religious dispositions is as straightforward as any that has been devised. Persons who are basically reflective apprehend God best by knowing him. Those who are more emotionally inclined find him by loving him. Those who are active by nature reach God by serving him, and contemplatives access him by meditating. All four of those aptitudes are present in each of us, but their proportions vary and it makes sense to lead with one's long suit.

To elaborate minimally:

Sufi poetry provides a brilliant instance of the approach to God through love, as does Rilke's *Book of Hours*. The intensely inward conversations with God in that book distill Rilke's search for an unmediated and intimate encounter with the heart of the universe, and biographical facts suggest that his lifelong devotion to Lou Andreas-Salome which was beginning at that time—a devotion that taught him that the holy can be found in physical human relationships as well as elsewhere—helped to power his spiritual quest. As for the Sufis, Rabi'a's celebrated night prayer to God is my all-time favorite.

> My God and my Lord: eyes are at rest, the stars are setting, hushed are the movements of birds in their nests, of monsters in the deep. And you are the Just who knows no change, the Equity that does not swerve, the Everlasting that never passes away. The doors of kings are locked and guarded by their henchmen, but your door is open to those who call upon you. My Lord, each lover is now alone with his beloved. And I am alone with you.

Turning from *bhakti* to *karma yoga*, from love to service, Mother Teresa comes immediately to mind as someone who found God through serving him; and (proceeding to *raja yoga*) I know contemplatives who experience God directly—wordlessly and without images—as a result of their prolonged practice of mental prayer.

My newest thought in this area, however, relates to *jnana yoga*, the way to God through knowledge, which happens to be my own primary bent. Such knowledge has nothing to do with factual information. It is an intuitive discernment, and my recent thought about it came through a sentence my eye chanced to fall upon. "There is certain kind of person," the sentence read, "who cannot truly pray without a pen in his hand."

That may sound bizarre to most people, but it makes perfect sense to me. For now and then it happens, that as I sit at my computer, straining to see some aspect of God's nature more clearly than ever before I have, I will glance out the window and, through the treetops and cloud formations that greet my eyes, illumination streams. A jubilation possesses me, and I feel myself touched by something divine.

A closing admonition: Finding God is not like finding a mislaid object, which ends the search. Gregory of Nyssa put this point definitively: "To seek God is to find him; to find God is to seek him."

ACKNOWLEDGMENTS

About halfway through the editing of this book I developed a painful tendinitis in both hands that made writing difficult and typing impossible. Not surprisingly, I started to panic and, I confess, despair that this project would ever see completion.

After feeling a little sorry for myself, I spoke with a Jesuit friend. "This book will never get written!" I said.

He thought for a few seconds and asked, "Whose book is it yours or God's?"

"If it's God's book," he continued, "it will get done. Maybe not on your timetable, but on God's."

He was right, of course. Not only did I have to hand over to God the success of this book, but also I had to rely on many friends, who helped me type dozens of letters and hundreds of pages. And so this book is very much a wonderful group project. As the angel says to Mary in the Gospel of Luke, "Nothing is impossible with God."

I would be remiss, then, if I didn't thank my Jesuit friends who helped me when my recalcitrant hands were unwilling to work: Jim Boynton, Matt Cassidy, Pablo Concha, Gabriel Côté, Chris Derby, Bob Gilroy, Dave Godleski, Tom Griffin, Ray Guiao, Steve Katsouros, Karl Kiser, Tom Lawler, Ned Mattimoe, Paul Nienaber, Charles O'Byrne, Bob O'Hare, Ross Pribyl, Tom Simonds, and George Williams. A special word of thanks goes to Liz Collier, who not only helped me with my typing but also when I dictated something she didn't care for, would turn to me and grimace. A good editor.

Thanks also to Tom Colchie, Rick Curry, David Donovan, George Drury, Caryl Johnson, and especially Pat Kossmann of Triumph Books, for their encouragement and advice. Thanks to my community at Bellarmine House in Cambridge for their support, as well as my Jesuit colleagues at *America* for their help and hospitality, especially George Hunt, Vinnie O'Keefe, Bob Collins, Dave Toolan, and John Donohue. Dan Wackerman and Kim Kowalski at *America* also helped with the typing of the final manuscript. Melinda Ruben, besides patiently proofing the final text, pointed out any terms or phrases that might have been unfamiliar to non-Christian readers. Thanks to my parents for proofing the final galleys. My Jesuit superiors, Jim Lafontaine and Bill Barry, were also most encouraging of a Jesuit scholastic who probably should have been studying theology instead of writing a book.

Most of all, I thank the people who generously took the time to respond to my question, and shared so much of their lives and their faith.

GLOSSARY

Included in this book are a number of names and phrases from various religious traditions that may be unfamiliar to readers. Some brief explanations are included here. For much of this information I am indebted to the following excellent sources: *The HarperCollins Dictionary of Modern Religion*, Jonathan Z. Smith, general editor; William Scott Green, associate editor; with the American Academy of Religion (1995), *The HarperCollins Encyclopedia of Catholicism*, Richard P. McBrien, general editor (1995), *Jewish Literacy* by Rabbi Joseph Telushkin (William Morrow, 1991), and *Islamic Spirituality: Foundations*, Seyyed Hossein Nasr, editor (Crossroad, 1987). For additional information about religious traditions, the best overall book remains Huston Smith's *The World's Religions: Our Great Wisdom Traditions* (HarperSanFrancisco, 1991).

Anselm, Saint (1033–1109) English monk, theologian, and archbishop of Canterbury. A prolific writer of letters, prayers, and theological works, he is well known for his *Proslogion*, which advanced the "ontological" argument for God's existence, and for his enduring description of theology as *fides quaerens intellectum*, "faith seeking understanding."

argument from design, cosmological argument. Two of the traditional philosophical "arguments" or "proofs" for the existence of God, and included in Saint Thomas Aquinas' "five ways" in his *Summa Theologica*. The argument from design attempts to demonstrate God's existence from the inherent and manifest order of the universe. The cosmological argument moves from the contingent, or dependent, character of the world to God as the noncontingent source. In other words, a "First Mover" is required to set all things in motion.

Baal Shem Tov (1700–1760) (Hebrew, "Master of the Good Name") Israel Ben Eliezer. Jewish leader, healer, and founder of Hasidism (from *Hasidim*, or "pious ones"), a religious renewal movement organized in Southern Poland and Ukraine, now found mostly in the United States and Israel. Because the world is full of God, the Baal Shem Tov believed that men and women should be joyful. His mission, he said, was to "stir the hearts of those seeking communion with God."

Baltimore Catechism, The Official text for religious instruction for Catholic children in the United States that was first published in 1885 and remained the standard text until the mid 1960s. *The Baltimore Catechism* was organized in a simple question-and-answer format.

Beatific Vision In Catholic theology, the direct knowing and loving of God, which comes after death, that is, the soul's final union with God.

Buber, Martin (1878–1965) Influential Jewish philosopher and theologian who, in his best-known work, *I and Thou*, argued that open and direct human relationships actualize and reveal God (the "Eternal Thou"). Buber was influenced by both Hasidism and existentialism.

Catherine of Siena, Saint (1347–1380) Mystic and writer. Catherine led an active life, throwing herself into the theological issues of the day. She played an important role in resolving the Great Schism of the fourteenth century. And she is one of only two women, along with Saint Teresa of Ávila, to be declared by the Catholic Church a "Doctor" of the Church, that is, an eminent teacher of the faith.

Catholic Worker movement Ministry for laypeople in service to the poor founded in 1933 by Dorothy Day (1897–1980) and Peter Maurin (1877–1949) in New York City. The movement continues to attract a wide variety of laypeople, and Catholic Worker "houses of hospitality" for the poor can be found across the country.

Chakra (Sanskrit, "wheels," "circles") In Hinduism and Buddhism, *chakras* are the centers of energy in the non-physiological body, lying along the spine. Each *chakra* is traditionally compared to a lotus flower with a set number of petals.

communio sanctorum (Latin, "communion of saints") In Christian theology, the great grouping of the faithful on earth, in purgatory, and in heaven, gathered together by the Holy Spirit.

Confessions Autobiography of Saint Augustine of Hippo (354–430). Part prayer, part life story, the *Confessions* are one of the foundational writings of Western culture. Its clear style and deeply personal approach to faith has influenced Christians since Augustine's time.

Dhammapada (Pali, *pada*, "footsteps"; *Dhamma*, "ultimate principle") Buddhist anthology of verse on a variety of topics, and one of the most popular Buddhist texts.

Dharma (Sanskrit, "bearing, supporting") In Buddhism, the proper course of conduct and action, ultimate realities and principles. *Dharma* is also used to express Buddhism as a system of thought and practice.

Emmaus In this New Testament story (Luke 24:13–35), Jesus Christ, after his Resurrection, appears to two of his disciples, who are still grieving his crucifixion and death. During their journey to Emmaus, a town near Jerusalem, Christ patiently explains his life's ministry, though "their eyes were kept from recognizing him." Later, as Christ breaks bread with the two, they suddenly recognize him. Just as suddenly, he disappears. The passage is sometimes used to illustrate how even believers can overlook Christ, or God, in their midst.

esse (Latin, "being") Often used in philosophical discourse, especially in Greek philosophy and medieval scholasticism. In scholastic philosophy, God's very essence is to be.

Gospel of Thomas Second century (A.D.) collection of sayings of Jesus supposedly transcribed by the apostle Thomas. The text, which did not win formal approval by the early Church, is not included in the New Testament and is therefore referred to as one of the "apocryphal" Gospels.

Gregory of Nyssa, Saint (335–395 A.D.) Bishop and theologian. One of the Cappadocian Fathers, who along with his brother Saint Basil the Great and friend Saint Gregory of Nazianzus, proclaimed the divinity of Christ, refuting the teachings of Arianism.

hadith qudsi (Arabic, "holy saying") In the Islamic tradition, one of a collection of sacred sayings communicated by God (Allah) through the Prophet Muhammad, though not included in the Quran. In a *hadith qudsi* God speaks in the first person through the Prophet. Also referred to as a Divine Saying.

Hazrat Inayat Khan (1882–1927) Indian teacher who was one of the first to bring Sufism to the West, traveling throughout Europe and the United States. In 1910 he established the Sufi Order of the West to help transmit an Islamic mysticism suitable for modern Western culture.

Hopkins, Gerard Manley (1844–1889) English Jesuit priest and poet. Hopkins was converted to Catholicism with the help of Cardinal John Henry Newman in 1866. His poetry, containing unusual rhythms and innovative wordplay, remained unpublished until 1918.

Ignatius of Loyola, Saint (1491–1556) Spanish mystic and founder of the Society of Jesus, commonly called the Jesuits. Ignatius, originally a soldier and courtier, decided to devote his life to the service of God after a series of mystical experiences in prayer. These experiences later became the basis for his influential handbook for spiritual growth, *The Spiritual Exercises*. In 1540 he started the Society of Jesus, a group of men founded to "help souls."

Kierkegaard, Søren (1813–1855) Danish philosopher considered by many to be the father of modern existentialism. Kierkegaard, a Lutheran, stressed in his writings the importance of personal decision as determinative of individual existence, the most important decision being that of faith. His writings include *Fear and Trembling* and *The Sickness Unto Death*.

Knights of Malta Catholic religious order founded in the twelfth century for hospital work and military service. Both laypersons and clerics are members of the group, which today focuses its ministry on hospital work.

Kundalini In Hinduism and Buddhism, *Kundalini* (Sanskrit "coiled one") represents the potent spiritual energy resting at the base of the spine.

Liturgy of the Hours In Catholic tradition, the daily prayers for praising God and sanctifying the day, consisting of an Office of Readings, Morning and Evening Prayer, Daytime Prayer, and Night Prayer. Also known as the Divine Office, and typically contained in a book called a breviary.

Lourdes French town where Catholics believe the Virgin Mary appeared to Saint Bernadette Soubirous, then a young girl, in 1858. Now a popular pilgrimage site.

Marcel, Gabriel (1889–1973) French existential philosopher known for his work in demonstrating the compatibility of faith and existentialism in such works as *Being and Having*.

Merton, Thomas (1915–1968) American Trappist monk, author, peace activist and mystic. Merton, who entered the Cistercian Order after a rather wild early life, became one of the most influential Catholic thinkers of his time and a prolific writer. His immensely popular autobiography, *The Seven Storey Mountain*, was published shortly after he entered the monastery of Our Lady of Gethsemani in Kentucky.

mezuzah (Hebrew, "doorpost") Small parchment on which is inscribed the first two paragraphs of the *Shema* (Deut. 6:4–9, 11:13–21), enclosed in a small case and affixed in the doorways of Jewish homes. The practice is done so in accordance with the precept of Deuteronomy 6:9. Traditionally, the *mezuzah* sanctifies the home and serves as a reminder of God's continual presence.

motzi (Hebrew, "to bring forth") Jewish prayer of blessing before a meal: "Blessed are you, Lord God, King of the universe, who brings forth bread from the earth."

Mount Calvary (Latin, *calvaria*, "skull") Traditional site of Jesus' Crucifixion, located outside the walls of Jerusalem. Calvary is the Latin translation of the Aramaic *Golgotha*, meaning "place of the skull."

Newman, John Henry (1801–1890) English cardinal and writer. Newman, one of the great Catholic thinkers of the 19th century, wrote prolifically explaining the Catholic faith. As Fellow of Trinity College at Oxford, he exerted a wide influence on English Catholics. His book *Apologia Pro Vita Sua* is a history of his religious opinions and beliefs.

Pascal, Blaise (1623–1662) French mathematician, scientist, and religious thinker. Pascal is credited with developing modern probability theory. His *Pensées*, a collection of notes explicating his ideas on Christianity, posited that God is finally known not by human efforts but through grace, not through reason but with the heart.

Pesach Seder (Hebrew, *Pesach*, "paschal lamb"; *seder*, "order") The Jewish home ritual that commemorates and relives the Passover experience as described in the Book of Exodus. The *seder* typically includes a meal and prayers setting the stage for the ritual, rhetorical questions concerning the unique nature of the evening, ritualized answers elaborating the Exodus experience, and *hallel*, a collection of joyous psalms in praise of God the Redeemer.

Plotinus (205–270 A.D.) Greek Neoplatonic philosopher. Plotinus' work, contained in his *Enneads*, focuses on the "One" (also called the "Good," or the "Universal Mind") from which all else flows, and to which the human soul ultimately returns by means of contemplation, moral action, and love for the One.

Rabi'a al-'Adawiyya Eighth-century Muslim woman saint and writer of Sufi love poetry. Emphasizing the Islamic doctrine of the affirmation of unity *(tawhid)*, Rabi'a wrote of God's love as the core of the universe.

Ramadan During this month, Muslims in good health observe a daytime fast, refraining from food, drink, smoking, and sexual activity. A breaking of the fast is enjoyed in early evening followed by traditional litanies in a mosque. A predawn meal is also eaten before the fast begins. Fasting is one of the "Five Pillars" of Islam.

Ramakrishna (1836–1886) Hindu mystic and inspiration for the Vedanta Society. The ascetic Ramakrishna, a devotee of the Hindu goddess Kali, believed that he had experienced the truths at the core of all religions, and that they were essentially the same.

Rule of Saint Benedict Sixth-century monastic "rule," or guidebook, written by Benedict of Nursia (480–547) containing both spiritual doctrine and practical advice. The *Rule* has served as one of the chief bases of monastic life to the present day.

Rumi (1207–1273) Jalal al-Din Rumi, the great Persian mystical poet and inspiration for the Mevlevi Dervish order. Rumi described Sufism as "To feel joy in the heart at the time of grief."

Sama Veda (Sanskrit, "knowledge of chants") Sacred Vedic Sanskrit text, arranged for chanting, containing verses from the *Rig Veda*, Hinduism's sacred text of hymns to various Hindu deities.

Shema Daily Jewish prayer affirming and blessing the oneness of God. The traditional name of the prayer is from the first word, in Hebrew, taken from Deuteronomy 6:4: "Hear, O Israel, the LORD is Our God, the LORD is One." (*Sh'ma Yisra'el, Adonai Eloheinu, Adonai Ekhah.*)

Sufism A general term referring to mystical traditions in Islam, stressing the inner dimension of the faith.

Sun Dance In Lakota tradition, a four-day ritual in which participants abstain from food and water, while performing rigorous religious rites, including the piercing of the flesh of the chest and back. These rites are also performed by other Plains groups, such as the Crows, Blackfeet, Cheyennes, and Arapahoe.

Sunday, Billy (1863–1935) William Ashley Sunday. American Presbyterian minister and evangelist whose sermons and religious "revivals" attracted enthusiastic crowds in the early part of the twentieth century.

Talmud (Hebrew, "study," "knowledge") The Jewish compilation of explanations and commentaries on the *Mishnah*, that is, the sixty-three tractates in which Rabbi Judah the Prince set down the Oral Law, around 200 A.D.

Tao Te Ching (Chinese, "The Book of the Way and the Power.") Earliest work of Taoist philosophy, authored by Lao-Tzu in the mid-fourth century B.C. Taoism is concerned with the concept of primordial unity, from which all things evolve and ultimately return.

Teresa of Ávila, Saint (1515–1582) Spanish nun, mystic, writer and reformer of the Carmelite order. Teresa founded her first reformed convent of the Discalced Carmelites in 1562 in Ávila, Spain. Her book *The Interior Castle* describes her experiences of mystical prayer. In 1970 she was declared the first woman Doctor of the Church.

Thérèse of Lisieux, Saint (1873–1897) As a young girl, Thérèse Martin entered the Carmelite monastery in Lisieux, France, where she would spend the remainder of her life. Her autobiography, *The Story of a Soul*, written at the request of her religious superiors at the monastery, is one of the spiritual classics of modern times. In her book she stressed her "little way" of finding God in daily life and in simple tasks.

Thomas Aquinas, Saint (1225–1274) One of the greatest Catholic theologians, Saint Thomas, a Dominican friar, wrote extensively on nearly all topics of theological and philosophical discourse, and is particularly well known for his thoughts on God's existence and natural law. He is the father of scholastic theology (his name gives rise to the term "Thomism"), and his magisterial *Summa Theologica*, a compilation of theology presented in a then novel question-and-answer form, is still used by theologians.

Vinaya Pitaka One of the three *pitakas* (Sanskrit, "basket" or "collection") of the three-part collections of Buddhist scriptures. The *Vinaya* ("rule") *Pitaka* is comprised of the history and commentary on Buddhist monastic life. *Vinaya* itself is a crucial part of the spiritual development of a Buddhist monk or nun and defines the order's communal life.

Women-Church Christian religious communities of women (though men are often included) that meet for worship together. The Women-Church communities are particularly interested in affirming the experience and place of women in the Christian churches and in society at large.

yoga (Sanskrit, "to yoke") In the Hindu religion, a method of training designed to lead to the integration of the human spirit with God. There are four *yogas*, or paths to God: *jnana*, the path to oneness through knowledge; *bhakti*, through love; *karma*, through work; and *raja*, through psychophysical exercises.

Zohar (Hebrew, *Sefer ha-Zohar*, "Book of Splendor") The most famous work of *kabbalah*, that is, the range of mystical activity in Judaism. The *Zohar*, which modern scholars believe to have been written around the thirteenth century, is written in the form of a commentary on the Torah.

About the Editor

James Martin, S.J., is a Jesuit scholastic studying at the Weston Jesuit School of Theology in Cambridge, Massachusetts, in preparation for ordination to the priesthood. As part of his Jesuit training, Mr. Martin worked for two years in Nairobi, Kenya, where he helped East African refugees to start small businesses, and eventually opened a shop that sold refugee-made handicrafts. After leaving Kenya, he spent one year as associate editor with *America* magazine, receiving two Catholic Press Association Awards for his writing. Before entering the Society of Jesus, Mr. Martin, a graduate of the University of Pennsylvania's Wharton School of Business, worked for six years in corporate finance and human resources.